Dan Rice

Brittanys

Everything About History, Purchase,
Care, Nutrition, Training, and Behavior

Filled with Full-color Photographs
Illustrations by Michele Earle-Bridges

BARRON'S

The Brittany, formerly known as the Brittany Spaniel, probably originated in the seventeenth century in the Brittany province of northwest France. That province was isolated from the rest of that country and was principally populated by British inhabitants, and thus was heavily influenced by Celtic culture. Whether British or French in origin, the Brittany was and is a consummate hunting dog.

Origin of the Canine Species

DNA evidence proves that wolves of various types were the progenitors of all domestic dogs, and Brittanys are no exception. Through-out history, dogs have served people in many roles. It is only natural that the dominant human beings should select and breed dogs of the size, strength, coat, and temperament that please them or fill their particular needs.

Selective Breeding

Dogs have an easily manipulated genetic structure, one that allows conformation changes to be easily altered by selective breeding. Dogs with the same genotype (genetic properties) have the capacity to vary in phenotype (visible

A typical Brittany displays an alert, intelligent, and curious expression.

and behavioral properties). Phenotypic changes are produced in nature by the interaction of genotype with the animal's environment. By choosing dogs that display certain traits, and by using only those dogs in a breeding program, many canine physical characteristics can be molded and readily changed. This process is known as selective breeding, which may or may not be the answer to the origin of the hundreds of breeds and the multitude of sizes, shapes, temperaments, and uses of dogs that presently populate the earth. It is certainly the method used to produce minor phenotypic changes such as behavior modification, various coat types, and color patterns that are seen within the Brittany breed.

A Rose by Any Other Name

Although the Brittany province of France—known in that country as Bretagne—is the apparent source of the Brittany's name, other

The Brittany's hunting skills are quickly recognized in the field.

evidence connects the name to Britannia, part of England rather than France. The paradox that surrounds the Brittany's name is no less confusing than the actual origin of the breed.

Until relatively recently, the official breed name was Brittany Spaniel. *Spaniel* literally means *Spanish dog*. Whether or not Spain had some hand in developing the Brittany is problematic. Spaniels, pointers, and setters may have all originated in Spain, and the name spaniel could be a corruption of *hispano* or *español*.

Regardless of the source of its name, the modern Brittany has the historical scenting

ability of the famous bird dogs of Europe. Its colors and general type are similar to the other setters, pointers, and spaniels of coastal France, Holland, England, Flanders, and Germany. Many of the bird-hunting dogs of Great Britain and Wales, notably the Welsh Springer Spaniel and some of the setters, are similar in appearance to the Brittany, and may share ancestry with it.

Pointers and setters are usually faster, leggier, lighter in weight, and have a wider hunting range than spaniels. As their name implies, they point at their quarry and attempt to keep it pinned down until the hunter can arrive within shooting distance. In those regards, the Brittany belongs to the pointer-setter types of hunting dogs, and it shares characteristics other than color and type with them. The Brittany is a scenting dog and an instinctive pointer with the ability to *set,* or hold, its quarry in cover.

Setting game birds predates easily accessible gunpowder and the sport of shooting. Ancient setters would scent a covey of birds, point them, and pin them down. The hunters would then throw large nets over the vegetative cover occupied by the birds, and the birds were thus captured alive. Similar setting techniques have been used more recently to capture wild game birds used in organized sport shooting. Setters were also quite efficiently used in hunting game birds with falcons. After the dogs pointed and set a covey of birds, the falcons were made ready, and when the game birds were flushed, the falcons attacked them in the air.

Training a Brittany to hunt with falcons is still being done in England.

Brittany History

The Brittany is one of Europe's oldest hunting breeds, but its specific ancestry is subject to debate. Since no written history is available prior to the mid-1800s, we must refer to paintings of the seventeenth century for descriptions and locations of earlier Brittanys.

Various references join the Brittany's ancestors with the Irish invaders of France. Those people were avid wildfowlers and brought with them the long-tailed Irish Red-and-White Setter. That breed dates from the eighteenth century, and is believed to be the progenitor of the Irish Setter as well. Some writers refer to English sportsmen who went to Brittany, France, to shoot woodcock. They often took along their English Setters, which might have been crossed

with a Breton, or dog that was native to Brittany. There is no question that the early Brittanys were sporting dogs, whether or not they shared origin with the Irish Setter centuries ago.

An English sportsman is said to have developed the earliest tailless Brittanys as woodcock hunters in France in about 1850. An imported, naturally bobtailed, lemon-and-white dog was bred to a mahogany-and-white native hunting bitch to produce those dogs. The Brittany as we know it today probably dates from those crosses.

Arthur Enaud, who lived in the valley of Douron, France, is principally responsible for the popular orange-and-white-colored Brittany. To fix these colors, to combat the degeneration that often accompanies inbreeding, and to increase the dogs' scenting abilities, Enaud is thought to have crossed the Italian Bracco and the Braque de Bourbonnais with his Brittanys. Braques had

This litter of six-week-old Brittany puppies are nearly ready for new homes.

terrific scenting ability and were developed as pointing breeds in France. The tailless characteristic of the Brittany was also more firmly fixed by the Braque de Bourbonnais, which possessed a naturally bobbed tail. The early French standards required that all Brittany puppies be born tailless, but that requirement was soon abandoned. The outcrosses mentioned are thought to be the last such mixing of breeds that occurred in the foundation of the Brittany. That also explains why a few of the Brittanys of today are born tailless.

The Brittany in America

The early American popularity of the Brittany was due in part to the influence of a Frenchman who lived in Veracruz, Mexico. J. Pugibet imported Brittanys from France to hunt in Yucatán, Mexico. A friend of Pugibet, Louis Thebaud, lived in New Jersey, but often hunted in Mexico as well. Thebaud was so impressed with

the dogs that he imported them into the United States. He established a Brittany breeding program with Eudore Chevier, a French Canadian who lived in Winnipeg, Manitoba. Thebaud helped form the Brittany Spaniel Club of North America, which merged with the American Brittany Club in 1942.

The Brittany has been recognized in the United States since the 1930s. From 1934 until 1982, the American Kennel Club (AKC) registered Brittanys as *Spaniel, Brittany*. It was known as the "world's only pointing spaniel," and was possibly classified as a spaniel because it characteristically worked within range of the hunter's gun, and would flush game birds in that range.

When the AKC recognized the first Brittany club, a petition was circulated to change the breed name from Brittany Spaniel to Brittany. The request was denied by the AKC because of the registration name in other countries, including the country of origin (whatever that might have been). But finally, on September 1, 1982, in response to the national breed club's request, the AKC dropped "spaniel" in spite of the nomenclature inconsistency with other countries, and the breed name was officially changed to Brittany. Elsewhere in the world, this breed continues to be called the Brittany Spaniel.

This name change seems well justified for several reasons, and why the Brittany was designated as a spaniel remains open to conjecture. The Brittany's conformation differs significantly from that of most spaniels in that it has a much lighter build. Its ears are shorter and set higher, and in general the Brittany is leggier than most spaniels. Its coat is not the heavy type that is characteristic of cockers or springers, and the spaniel is basically a flushing dog, whereas the Brittany is a pointer.

The Brittany's short bobbed tail is characteristic of the breed.

Brittany field trial competition in the United States has always been held with the pointers and setters, to which the Brittany is similar in form and function (phenotype), and not with spaniels or other water-retrieving dogs. Therefore, the revised breed name seems to fit the Brittany in every respect.

Early Show History

Brittanys were first exhibited at the Paris dog show of 1900 and official French recognition of the breed came in 1905 when an orange-and-white male was registered in France under the official breed name *l'épagneul Breton*, or its English equivalent, Brittany Spaniel.

French shows thereafter had entries of at least 75 Brittanys. As a show dog, the Brittany improved in type and uniformity in the early 1900s. By 1925 more than 100 Brittanys were entered in the show at Rennes, France. The dog shows of that era and beyond were instrumental in preserving many breeds that otherwise would have become extinct. Breeds and strains were saved by fanciers and were exhibited in dog shows. The depressed economy of that period of European history dictated that only the best of these dogs were kept as breeding stock.

SOUND BITE

The American Kennel Club recognized the Brittany in 1934 as a spaniel, then changed its name to Brittany in 1982.

APPRECIATING THE BRITTANY

A Brittany is ideally suited for the role of hunting assistant or house pet. Practically every Brittany possesses remarkable pointing and retrieving skills in the field, yet has family companion dog qualities that are equally important. A typical Brittany is affectionate, loyal, obedient, and trainable. The Brittany is indeed a dog that has it all!

Dual-Purpose Dog

"Dual purpose" implies that in the Brittany breed there are few or no differences in conformation, intelligence, strength, and scenting or retrieving ability between field trial dogs and conformation show dogs. A good Brittany has the disposition of the best house pet and companion, yet retains a passion for hunting. The American Brittany Club and Brittany breeders of the United States have committed themselves to preserving the Brittany as a multipurpose dog. Many sporting breeds have started out with similar intentions, but over the years have shown a definite split in appearance and purposes.

This beautiful Brittany is equally comfortable in a companion or hunting role.

A true dual-purpose dog can leave the field one day, have a bath, and win in a conformation show the next day. That implies that concerned Brittany breeders must support and compete in both phases of the fancy. The result is that a field Brittany maintains the same coat, movement, temperament, and size as conformation show dogs.

The Versatile Brittany

Brittany fanciers have always recognized the intelligence, soundness, balance, and symmetry of motion in their breed, and continue to value and cultivate those features in their hunting and conformation dogs. By comparison with other breeds, the Brittany isn't a *pretty* dog. It is difficult to judge the vibrant color and airy,

On point in the field, this Brittany displays the beauty and form for which it was bred.

flowing grace of an Irish Setter against the quick, productive movement of a Brittany. It's probably for those reasons that the Brittany has not won its fair share of "Best in Group" or "Best in Show" awards. However, this oversight is more than compensated for by the fact that the Brittany has produced more dual champions than any other breed: 508 were recognized as of December 2006.

After its introduction into the United States, the Brittany has changed slowly in popularity and acceptance. The AKC registered 14,901 Brittanys in 1992, making them twenty-eighth in popularity. Those numbers have been reduced by nearly half; 7,853 were registered in 2005. They are now thirtieth in AKC canine popularity and eighth in popularity among the AKC hunting breeds. This loss in general popularity is not necessarily a negative sign for Brittany fanciers and breeders.

Brittanys are often housed and hunted together.

At home, your Brittany continues to practice by pointing backyard songbirds.

Gundog

The Brittany is an outstanding performance dog with a fantastic nose and superb hunting style. With those attributes it's no wonder that the breed is one of the most esteemed hunting dogs in America today. The Brittany is a medium-sized dog with an acute sense of smell and an excellent retrieving instinct. Because its natural pointing instinct is easily developed, the Brittany is a fine choice as an upland bird-hunting dog.

The Brittany is quickly trained and with a minimum of practice will become a superb woodcock or grouse hunter. The Brittany will retrieve waterfowl from ponds and streams, and like the spaniels, pointers, and setters, it uses windborne scents to locate its quarry.

In the field, a Brittany works well in any terrain and in most climates. It endures the cold very well, and can be trained to hunt hare as well as partridge and other upland birds. It is a strong, lively, energetic hunter that rarely lacks endurance.

The Brittany's primary popularity in the United States has come from hunting and field trial enthusiasts and weekend bird hunters. This is a bird dog that typically quarters closely in the field, making it quite adaptable to today's limited shooting areas. It is highly trainable, and is a natural, soft-mouthed retriever. The Brittany is truly a dog for all hunters. It has been called the apartment dweller's weekend gundog, and may well serve such a purpose.

Although some Brittanys are hunted as early as six months of age, they probably reach their prime between four and five years. They are clever, biddable dogs that show very little stubbornness in the field.

Family Dog

For those who are not interested in hunting but do appreciate the active qualities and temperaments of hunting dogs, the beautiful Brittany easily adapts to a life of dog shows or romping with the kids. Its size makes it desirable as an urban backyard pet. It is a great companion for the jogger or runner and is capable of carrying a moderate-sized pack. It is a healthy, happy dog that is playful and trustworthy and loves children.

A Brittany is a superb family dog—loyal and faithful whether in the hunting field or the backyard. It is unique among sporting dogs because its coat is relatively short, dense, flat, or wavy, never excessively feathered, and doesn't require extensive grooming and trimming.

Lack of self-confidence is not a characteristic of the breed, although unthinking adults and improperly instructed children can cause that trait to develop. Because the Brittany is sensitive and must be patiently handled, it is sometimes described as a timid dog. However, meekness and doubt aren't adjectives that are used to describe the energetic and playful Brittany. It is typically a gentle dog, loving, happy, and fun to have around. Brittany breeders describe their dogs as friendly and nonaggressive. In that light, they may appear timid to the uninformed. They are easy dogs to housebreak and make great kids' pets. They are characteristically inquisitive, intelligent, and get along well with other pets.

The Brittany is a bright, intelligent dog that is anxious to please its owners, as this quote from a breeder with more than 25 years of experience indicates: "A Brittany would die for you! These dogs love life and people and want to do anything to please you. They are sensitive and highly manipulative, and sometimes are smarter than their owners, so they are best placed with intelligent, friendly, well-informed, and active families."

The friendly Brittany doesn't respond well to rough treatment, and force-training measures should not be used. That doesn't mean that the Brittany can't tolerate correction. It is a strong, tough dog with a gentle disposition and a great heart, and its best home is with active, even-tempered, and patient owners.

Think Before You Buy

The Brittany's exceptional qualities do not necessarily make it an ideal dog for everyone. Its heritage is that of a sporting field dog, meaning that it shouldn't be compared with small house pets that require minimal exercise or attention. Because your Brittany is an active, high-energy dog, your time and a fair amount space must be provided for it to expend that energy. You should never purchase any dog on a whim, least of all a Brittany. Unless you lead an active outdoor life and plan to spend a great deal of time with your new Brittany, maybe you should rethink your selection.

A Brittany focused on its handler's signal.

SELECTING YOUR BRITTANY

A Brittany puppy will share your home and heart for many years. It will become another member of your family, emanating and needing love and requiring training. It will be a major investment of your time and money that should be cared for as any other valuable addition to your family.

Are You Ready for a Dog?

Impulse buying often leads to disappointment and is usually disastrous when purchasing a pet. Ask yourself a few questions before acquiring any dog. A simplified checklist follows that contains many items to consider before acquiring a new dog.

✔ Has the purchase of a dog been discussed with every member of your family?

✔ Is there sufficient spare time in your life for an animal that requires your love, regular training and grooming, and lots of attention?

✔ Will you take responsibility for its care? You have the final vote and you must personally assume the accountability for your dog's well-being.

✔ Are you prepared to furnish the new puppy adequate housing? In most cases, that means

This beautiful Brittany is a natural pointer, whether working or playing.

a fenced yard and ready access to your home—or at least a warm, dry doghouse.

✔ Are you aware of the true, ongoing cost of dog ownership, which includes purchase price, veterinary care, food, parasite control, dishes, toys, training aids, bed, collars, and leashes?

✔ Have you calculated the expense of training if you want to enter field trial, agility, or obedience competition?

✔ Have you investigated boarding kennels or do you have reliable friends who will care for your Brittany when you aren't able to do so?

Timing

Planning is important. In order to start a pup out correctly, everyone in the family should be in a settled routine. Consider these factors:

• Confusion reigns in most households during the holiday season, and a puppy's needs may be lost in the rush. There are many events that take a great deal of your time during that busy

Brittanys love gentle, kind, and affectionate children.

period. Don't add one more! Instead, purchase the Brittany's equipment to place under the Christmas tree and bring the puppy home later

---

TIP

Responsible Care

Grownups often make the mistake of delegating a puppy's care to a four- or five-year-old child, but that is a serious judgment error. Children that age are too young for that responsibility. A puppy needs you, your time, attention, love, and direction in order to mature into a well-mannered dog, a pet that you will be proud to have in your home.

---

when your family will have more time to focus on the new Brittany.

• Does your family usually take a seasonal trip? If you plan to be gone the first few weeks of July, don't bring a new pup home in May or June. Wait until after the household is quiet and the usual routine is established before you tackle housebreaking and leash training. It is a mistake to start those efforts, then let them lapse or pass them off to someone else.

• Shop for a puppy after spring break if your home is going to be filled with friends or relatives during that time. Extra people to play with the pup might seem like a good idea, but more likely they will be counterproductive and upset your training program.

Is a Brittany the Dog for You?

There were 2,513 Brittany litters registered by the AKC in 2005. That number has decreased slightly but has remained relatively constant for the last decade, which indicates a continued interest in the breed in the United States, but not an oversupply of puppies. When breeds become high in popularity, they often attract too much attention and are overbred. The Brittany hasn't risen to that popularity height yet, and let's hope it never will. Responsible breeders still maintain good control over the Brittany's numbers.

Health and Life Expectancy

Among the smaller hunting breeds Brittanys are generally healthy dogs and are usually destined to live rather long lives. It is common to have your Brittany for a dozen years, and some reach the age of 14 or 15.

The ways to ensure good health and longevity for a Brittany aren't much different from our own. First and foremost, it is critically important to purchase your Brittany puppy from a reliable breeder who screens for hereditary health. That screening includes having both of the puppy's parents examined for the kinds of genetic problems that are seen in Brittanys.

Extremely important is to practice a preventive medicine program, including parasite control, which is followed throughout life. Proper nutrition is equally important to your pet's longevity. Practice commonsense protection, which begins with confinement to a backyard or kennel. Activity and grooming plans are fundamental to a dog's general health. Brittanys are inquisitive, intelligent pets and special attention should be given to keeping them as busy as possible.

Exercise may not be a problem if you hunt—but if your hunting is done only for a few hours on an occasional October weekend, it may not supply enough exercise for your Brittany. In the case of a companion pet, you must arrange regular playtimes or your Brittany will become melancholic or bored and will develop nuisance habits such as chewing or digging. Separation anxiety is another possibility for a Brittany that is ignored and receives too little personal attention. (See discussion on page 34.) Walks with the dog and regular play and grooming times can't be overdone.

Veterinary Consultation

In choosing the right Brittany for your family, consult with knowledgeable people. Talk with a local veterinarian about your choice. In all probability, he or she has had experience with Brittanys and will be able to provide insights into your selection. A veterinarian's opinion is invaluable because she or he handles dozens of dogs of many different breeds every day, and has first-hand experience with the idiosyncrasies of many breeds.

A prepurchase discussion with your veterinarian serves many purposes:
• You will receive a general idea of the expense involved in routine Brittany care.
• The veterinarian can offer ideas about proper housing as well as boarding kennels in your area.
• He or she will address the risks of certain diseases that are indigenous to your region of the country.
• Your veterinarian will discuss hereditary conditions that occur in the Brittany.
• She or he will advise you of signs and symptoms of common problems.
• Your veterinarian may be able to recommend Brittany breeders, owners, and trainers in your locality.

Choosing the Right Brittany

Male or Female?

The sex of your pet is largely a matter of personal preference. Some people like the temperament of females, and others prefer masculine characteristics. There is very little difference between the sexes when seeking a Brittany that is to be neutered at or before adulthood.

In some breeds, either the male or female is more dominant than the other, but that is not a strong characteristic in Brittanys. Females are often gentler than males, but that is also relative. Hunting is a strong hereditary influence,

This new Brittany pup is investigating its strange new backyard.

and eagerness to work and play is a feature of both sexes. Either sex is loyal, trainable, affectionate, playful, and energetic.

If you choose a female, the cost of spaying might be a bit higher than the cost of neutering a male, but when prorated over the life of the dog, it is a minor consideration. The Brittany—whether male or female—is quick to learn, eager to please, and requires a minimum of correction.

Note: If your Brittany is spayed or neutered, there is no appreciable difference in the health care of dogs of either sex. However, if you are considering showing your Brittany, it must not be spayed or neutered. Be advised that intact females come in heat approximately every six months. You can enjoy hunting, obedience, agility, and 4-H competition with a spayed or neutered Brittany.

Appropriate Age of Puppy

Brittany dams often wean (stop feeding their puppies) by six weeks of age, but puppies learn to socialize with their dam and siblings while

still in the nest. Valuable lessons are taught during this time about getting along with other dogs, and it is a serious mistake to remove them from their nest before six or seven weeks. Most breeders keep puppies until they are seven to ten weeks old. You should try to bring the pup into your home as early as possible following that period for the following reasons:

• Bonding, the primary dog-human socialization period of puppies, is strongest from approximately three weeks to three months of age. It is during this important bonding time that the Brittany puppy should be introduced to your family.

• The new puppy will learn the "pack structure" of its human family.

• Good manners, such as housebreaking, are taught more easily at a young age.

• Puppies will more readily accept leash training when very young.

• Both good and bad habits are easily learned and those habits are deeply imprinted on a puppy's mind.

If that time passes by and you aren't able to bring the pup home before it is three months old, choose a puppy that has been handled as much as possible. Find a breeder who raises her

TIP

Acclimation

The best pet is one that has been regularly handled by the breeder's family from shortly after birth until eight weeks of age.

An anxious puppy wearing a new training collar anticipates further instruction.

Brittanys in a home environment, preferably one with children who handle the pups often. Puppies that mature without human companionship and are kept exclusively with other dogs may not readily bond with their owners and may be poor companions. However, Brittanys are very human-oriented dogs, and with love and attention, an adult Brittany will usually bond with an attentive and caring family. They are among the breeds that are most easily adopted as adults from shelters.

Temperament

Temperament differences in a litter of frisky puppies are difficult to discern, but the puppy's parents will often give you a clue about what their offspring's attitude will be like as a grown-up. Timidity or viciousness is not a typical trait of the Brittany, and you should not accept a puppy whose sire or dam is shy, unfriendly, or difficult to handle. Shy puppies usually will be more difficult to train and handle and often do not make good hunters or pets.

Type of Brittany

Contrary to the desire of the American Brittany Club (ABC), some Brittany breeders specialize in producing gundogs (shooting dogs) or field trial prospects. Those Brittanys are not a different variety from companion dog or conformation show Brittanys. However, they may be bred primarily from proven gundogs, with more regard to their field potential than their conformation. Talk to Brittany owners of shooting dogs and be sure that you are on the right track.

Gundogs

When choosing a field Brittany, similar guidelines should be employed as when choosing a companion or show dog, but with a few added requirements. Gundogs usually will be exposed to gunshots at a fairly early age, and certainly before they are sold as hunting prospects. They should have a keen inherent interest in retrieving, and at six to 12 weeks of age they should pick up and carry a ball, dummy, sock, or a bird wing.

Potential gundog puppies can't be critically evaluated based on their retrieving interest or ability. Most Brittanys will perform those functions whether or not they are the progeny of proven shooting dogs. Probably the most

This Brittany is becoming adjusted to water retrieving.

reliable measure of a hunting Brittany at the age of eight or ten weeks is the field performance of its parents and grandparents.

Field Trial Dogs

If you wish to locate a Brittany to compete in formal field trials, it's best to seek better advice than can be found in any book. Talk to individuals who are involved with field trials. Take their counsel regarding kennels that have routinely raised winning field trial Brittanys. Seek out the advice of successful professional trainers. Attend field trials and talk to the participating people. Scrutinize the personality and disposition of field trial Brittanys. The AKC or ABC can refer you to competition field trials in your region.

If you are considering field trial competition, be sure you understand the extent of training and practice that is necessary. Field trial dogs must receive nearly daily training and practice to perform at their best.

Conformation Show Dogs

Conformation show dogs will probably be available from the same kennels that produce field trial or weekend hunting dogs. However, you will have a better than average chance of acquiring a winning show dog from a breeder who has ribbons and rosettes from AKC shows hanging on the walls.

Out of every litter of Brittanys from champion "show" parents, perhaps only one or two puppies are destined to have a viable career as a show dog. The breeder often keeps the best puppies until they are three or four months of age to watch their development. There really shouldn't be any notable difference between show-quality puppies and gundogs. Kennels that raise field dogs should be able to supply your need for a show dog, and vice-versa.

Companion Dogs

It seems a shame to consign a wonderful hunting dog to a backyard where it never has the opportunity to point or retrieve game, but the Brittany doesn't seem to mind. These dogs have been bred for generations to hunt, but like most other hunting breeds, their personalities are malleable and they will adapt to the lifestyle of a family pet quite well and without problems. Some experts suggest that a Brittany puppy from field trial parents is often nervous and high-strung and doesn't do well as a family pet, but that premise is unproven.

A responsible Brittany breeder will likely have a few pet Brittanys to sell, because every litter includes some pups that don't quite measure up to the requirements of competition show or hunting dogs. A puppy's pedigree may be stippled with conformation champions that indicate careful breeding, but perhaps a puppy has a color or conformational fault that isn't conducive to a successful performance career. Such a pup is usually sold for less than the choice puppies, but it will have all the characteristics of those pups.

Finding the Right Breeder

Breeders can be located in any number of ways. The ABC is a fine place to start. Write to this organization at the address found in the back

A Brittany youngster being readied for field training.

of this book or contact its secretary by e-mail and ask for a list of Brittany breeders in your area. The AKC Internet site (http://www.AKC.org) provides links to ABC, its secretary, and other information about Brittanys.

Go to a conformation dog show in your part of the country to meet avid Brittany fanciers. Attend field trials, hunting tests, and agility trials, where you can make contacts that are invaluable if you are looking for a performance dog. Various dog magazines usually carry advertisements for Brittanys. Information about shows and trials can be obtained from the *American Kennel Club Gazette*, a monthly publication of the AKC that also contains a breed listing with many kennel advertisements. *The American Brittany*, a monthly magazine published by the ABC, is an excellent source of contacts.

A fine dual-purpose Brittany is at ease in any environment.

Look for Brittany ads in your local newspaper—but beware! Legitimate breeders may indeed advertise in newspapers, but a newspaper ad also may represent a backyard breeder or puppy mill operator, neither of whom is truly interested in the betterment of the breed.

Puppy mills own bitches of various breeds and produce hundreds of pups a year. They are notorious for producing poor-quality pups of questionable health and heritage. It's easy to spot a puppy factory. When you arrive, a litter may be presented without the dam. If you ask to see her, an excuse is made, or if you do see her, she is often in pitiful condition. If you gain entrance to the kennel, you will usually see various breeds, crowded, dirty conditions, very little provision for exercise, and thin, overworked dams. Puppy mills should be avoided at all costs.

Pet shops may be a viable option for you, but they won't have the pup's dam, and rarely will you see the puppy's siblings. A few such shops, however, provide pedigrees and records of their puppies' origins, thereby enabling you to learn the name of the kennel in which the pup was raised and thus satisfy your requirements.

Amateur breeders are improbable sources of reliable Brittanys. Before you buy a dog from a backyard breeder, be sure to carefully examine the AKC registration and pedigree of the dam and sire. If the litter isn't properly registered, beware! Backyard-bred puppies are often less expensive because their parents are often of questionable heritage and are rarely screened for genetic faults. Puppies from a union of two pet Brittanys may possibly prove to be fine pets, but it is unlikely that you will receive a guarantee of any kind.

Health Records

You have found what you believe to be the perfect puppy, a bundle of energy that is active and healthy. There are several documents that should accompany your new Brittany. Reputable breeders will have this information readily available, and probably more. Be sure you receive all of it in writing. Among these documents are:

• The breeder's guarantee that the puppy is in good health, along with written documentation of any special terms that apply to the purchase, such as an agreement to spay or castrate the pup by a certain age. The duration of the guarantee should be noted and how it is to be fulfilled. Most breeders will replace a pup if it has a disease or deformity that is discovered by your veterinarian within a few days of purchase. Be sure that the terms of the guarantee clearly specify whether it assures you of your money back, or a replacement pup.

• The date(s) of health examinations, and the name and address of the veterinarian who performed the examination(s).

• A record of when and by whom the pup was vaccinated, the product used, and when another vaccination is needed.

• The date a worm check was done and the results of that fecal exam.

• The date of treatment for the parasites if the fecal exam was positive, the name of the product that was administered, and the dose used.

• A record of any illness suffered by your puppy as well as the name and dosage of medication(s) used.

• If a heartworm, tick, or flea preventive program has been started, the dates and product(s) used and instructions for continuation.

• The pup's diet should be documented, including the quantity of food, brand name, and frequency of feeding.

Registration of Your Brittany

If your Brittany's parents are registered with the AKC, you should receive an AKC litter registration application at the time you pay for the puppy. You and the breeder should carefully complete every space in the application, paying special attention to the type of registration you seek. Then submit it to the AKC with the proper fee. Exceptions to this rule are:

1. If you are buying a pet-quality pup, the breeder may withhold the registration papers until proof of neutering is furnished.

2. If you pay for the pup in installments, registration papers may be withheld until the final payment is received.

3. The registration type should be marked "full," unless you agree to a *limited* registration.

A dog with an AKC Limited Registration is not eligible to be entered in an AKC breed competition in a licensed or member dog show. It is eligible, however, to be entered in any other event, such as obedience, tracking, field trials, hunting tests, and agility. Limited Registration is determined only by the litter owner(s) and can be changed to Full Registration only by the litter owner(s). The litter owner(s) must obtain and submit an AKC Application to Revoke Limited Status, which then is completed and sent to the AKC with the processing fee. After processing, the AKC will send a Full Registration certificate to the dog's new owner.

If no AKC registration application is available from the breeder, you are in a dangerous buyer-beware situation. The AKC is not a regulatory agency. It can't enforce guarantes of any kind and isn't responsible for fraudulent information received. You might need to resort to small-claims court for satisfaction. If you are still determined to buy the pup, be sure to get a bill of sale from the breeder, which contains the name and AKC registration numbers of the litter, sire, and dam, the dates of breeding, the date of whelping, and the names and phone numbers of the owners of both sire and dam. This information may be good only as a keepsake, and won't necessarily help you register your Brittany.

A pedigree is a record of several of the puppy's ancestors. It has no particular value for pet Brittanys, but is very significant if you have purchased a competition dog. If the breeder doesn't prepare a pedigree, one is available from the AKC for a fee if you are able to furnish the AKC litter registration number or the permanent registration number of your new puppy.

HOW-TO: CHOOSE A

Judging Health

When confronted with half a dozen happy, wriggling, tail-wagging little puppies, it is difficult to concentrate on health issues, but it is important that you do so before you choose your Brittany pup. Inspect the available puppies and make a rough evaluation of the health, personality, and conformation of each one before it is chosen to share your home.

Remember, bad breeding rarely yields good pups. If you see a collection of skinny, runny-eyed, lethargic, coughing puppies, don't handle them! Run, don't walk, to the nearest exit. Don't make the mistake of taking a sick pup home for a trial, with a guarantee that it will get better in a day or two. Don't take the responsibility of buying a pup

With the pup on your lap, check its bite, nose, eyes, abdomen, and tail for abnormalities.

that is receiving medication. Raising a healthy, active puppy is sufficient challenge without buying more trouble. Everyone is entitled to begin his or her relationship with a healthy dog—don't settle for less!

The Puppy's Parents

Begin your breeder contact by looking at both of the pup's parents if they are available. Your pup is a reflection of those adult dogs. If only the dam is owned, ask to see a picture of the sire, and if possible, pictures of his previous progeny. Don't rule out the litter because of the dam's physical condition, because most bitches look a bit rundown after weaning a litter of puppies. A good dam produces so much milk for the puppies that she is nutritionally drained after about six or eight weeks. She may be saggy, thinner than normal, and in poor coat when you see her. However, she should be clean and brushed, active and inquisitive. If available, look at her puppies from previous litters.

The personality of the dam and sire is a vital part of puppy selection. If the adults are shy, timid, or reluctant to be handled, their puppies will probably have similar attitudes.

On-the-Spot Evaluation

Assuming that you are looking at puppies that are eight to ten weeks old, you won't notice every possible fault, but you will make a more intelligent choice if you follow these guidelines.

✔ Stand back and observe the litter from a few yards away. If all tumbling and play stops when you enter the room and the puppies are reluctant to be picked up, they may be too young or not socialized to humans. If most run to hide behind their dam or nesting box, they are probably insecure and shouldn't leave their dam and siblings. Visit the litter a week later; if the pups still seem timid, perhaps you should be looking elsewhere.

✔ Seek a puppy that is inquisitive and affectionate but isn't aggressively attacking its siblings. Concentrate on puppies that don't hang back but are anxious to meet you. A certain amount of fear is normal in a puppy when a stranger approaches, but you shouldn't choose a pup that is overly shy.

✔ After you have narrowed the selection process to one or two puppies, squat or sit on the floor and carefully pick the puppy up. It is important to make yourself as small as possible when you first approach a pup. Lying on the floor (if practical) is an excellent posture. Don't grab a puppy as it runs by, and don't corner it somewhere. If the breeder's family has handled the pups, it will catch you; you won't have to chase it.

Caution: Reject a pup that immediately takes a defensive stance when you reach for it. If it snaps, screams, or otherwise seems frightened, it is definitely not the pup for you.

✔ Take the puppy into another room, away from the rest of the litter, and sit on the floor and watch its attitude when you relax your hold. If one end is still wagging and the other is licking your fingers or chin, you are nearing a good selection.

✔ Cradle the puppy in your arms in an upside-down position and gently rub its tummy and chin. It should let you do that with little objection and without squirming to immediately right itself.

✔ After you have made friendly overtures to the puppy, stay settled on the floor and put the pup on your lap. While petting it, open its mouth gently for a few seconds to check its bite. The upper incisor teeth should overlap and touch the lower front teeth (scissors bite). Any amount of gap between the upper and lower incisors (overshot or undershot) is a serious fault in the Brittany and should affect your choice, especially if you are looking for a dog to show. A slight bite fault should not be a consideration if the puppy is purchased as a pet and will be neutered. It can still be hunted and entered in several competitions. Its minor mouth deformity won't interfere with eating, and it rarely causes any health problems.

✔ With the puppy standing or sitting, feel its abdomen for evidence of an umbilical hernia, which will appear as a protrusion of tissue about the size of a marble at the site of the navel.

Getting down to the pup's eye level often means getting your face washed.

When the puppy is seven or eight weeks old, hernias are soft and, when pressed, may disappear into the abdomen.

✔ If selecting a male, check his scrotum for the presence of testicles. They should be descended into the scrotum by eight or ten weeks of age; if not, they might never descend. Either leave the pup with the breeder until the testicles drop into place, or pick another pup.

✔ Look at the puppy's eyes. A Brittany's eyes should not be "popped," or protruding. They should be clear, free of discharge, and the pup should not be squinting. At seven to eight weeks of age, the Brittany's eyes may still be blue. Brittany puppies may be six to eight months old before the dark amber eyes appear. As a rule of thumb, if the iris margin is dark, the iris will eventually become dark.

✔ The Brittany has a brown, tan, or dark pink nose-rubber that should be moist. Dry nostrils with matter caked in the corners are sure signs of health problems.

✔ A show dog puppy's tail may be naturally bobbed or surgically shortened, but it should be short. A tail of more than 4 inches (10.7 cm) in length is penalized in dog shows. A totally tailless Brittany is preferable to one with too long a tail.

TAKING YOUR BRITTANY HOME

A new puppy is your responsibility and you must make adjustments to your lifestyle to accommodate your new family member. Prepare for nighttime calls to the backyard, feeding schedules, playtime, grooming, and, of major importance, training time.

A visit to your veterinarian is strongly advised when you first acquire a new puppy, even if your Brittany seems to be in perfect health. The veterinarian will advise you on the appropriate timing of future booster vaccinations, as well as other preventive measures that will guard your pet's health.

Note: We have arbitrarily assigned names to your Brittany and used them in alternate chapters. "Jill" is the female, and "Chip" is the male.

First Days in Your Home

Jill must be fed several meals per day at regular intervals. She must be taken outside for eliminations several times a day. You must make allowances for her exercise needs,

This Brittany puppy is about to become a lifetime companion of some lucky person.

and those should include walks and playtimes. The new physical and emotional demands she makes of you may not always be enjoyable.

Diet

The records you received with your Brittany contain dietary information that lists the name of the food, the frequency of meals, and the quantity that is fed at each meal.

When you take Jill home, minimize the stress of environmental change by following the breeder's feeding program. Even if you decide to change her diet to a better-quality food, that change shouldn't be made immediately. After a week or two, you can begin desirable dietary changes. Make changes slowly by mixing the new product in gradually increasing amounts with the previously fed diet. A total dietary change should take at least a week or perhaps longer.

Necessary Quarters

As a family pet your new Brittany puppy will want to spend a good deal of time inside your house. Perhaps you already have a fenced yard and expect her to have the run of it and sleep in your home at night. Those accommodations are fine, provided you have taken a few preliminary precautions to protect both your puppy and your property.

Kennel and Run

A tightly fenced backyard will suffice for playing and training, but keep in mind that Brittanys are social animals that rarely exercise alone. You must initiate playtime. A run can be used to confine Jill when she can't be with you, and it should be large enough for her to move about freely. It serves no purpose other than as a protective confinement and place to sleep if she isn't allowed in the house. If you live in an area where snow or rain prevails, you should provide a cover for the run to help keep it dry. If in hot, dry country, a sunscreen is essential.

Buy or build a doghouse that is large enough to accommodate a full-grown Brittany. The dome-shaped, igloo types and the conventional rectangular fiberglass houses both have removable bottoms to facilitate cleaning. An igloo is insulated to be cooler in the summer and retain warmth in the winter.

Naturally, if Jill sleeps in your home, elaborate outdoor housing is unnecessary. If your backyard fence is only 3 feet (1 m) tall, it's not adequate to contain an energetic and adventuresome adult Brittany. If Jill is left alone behind a short fence, boredom or loneliness may stimulate her to jump.

Crate Training

Many owners can't imagine confining a sporting dog to a crate, but if used properly, the crate is an excellent and harmless way to manage your Brittany. It can be used after Jill has reached adulthood, but you should never keep her in a crate for extended periods of time. Most dogs enjoy the safety and cavelike atmosphere of a crate when sleeping, and a crate often makes dogs welcome in motel rooms when you are traveling.

Obtain a large fiberglass or molded plastic crate that has adequate ventilation. Don't make the mistake of buying a crate to fit a puppy; your dog will outgrow it in just a few months. Place in the crate an expendable, unwashed sock that you have worn, a blanket or rug, and a chew toy. When confining Jill to the crate, simply put her inside and walk away without comment, paying no attention to her complaints. If she barks, respond with a sharp *"No!"*

These easygoing Brittanys enjoy their owners' weekends at the lake.

and continue with your work. Never leave her in the crate for extended periods, and be sure to take her out of it frequently for eliminations.

In the beginning, confine Jill to the crate for only a few minutes. Gradually progress to an hour or two, and always leave the crate open when it isn't being used. Put her crate beside your bed and within a week she will happily spend the night in it, where she can be near her favorite person.

Regular sessions of crating will result in Jill's acceptance of the crate as her personal den, and she will soon return there for naps or when household activity becomes irritating, because it is quiet and secluded and keeps her out of reach when she wishes to be. It is also a great help when traveling, and is preferable to a seatbelt to control Jill in the backseat of your car. Never use the crate as a punishment for doing something wrong.

Always make entering the crate a positive experience and she won't resent it. Give her some special treat when she enters the crate but none when she is taken out. Don't make it appear that leaving the crate is something she should wish for. When you take her from the crate, open the gate, turn, and walk away without making a fuss over her.

Bonding and Socialization

Jill will form lifelong relationships with her human companions (commonly known as bonding) during the brief period of puppyhood. If you obtain her between the ages of six weeks and three months, she will accept correction quickly and easily. The lessons she learns will be promptly imprinted on her personality, and that is also the prime time to reciprocate her love and devotion.

Crating your Brittany for safety while on a trip makes good sense.

Tip: Bonding requires three factors: your Brittany, you, and loads of time. If you are too busy to devote regular and frequent time to the project, buy a nice goldfish instead of a Brittany.

Jill will quickly recognize her place in the family as well as the restrictions placed upon her, and she will seek ways to please you. She will learn to recognize her toys and to anticipate the ball games and hide-and-seek games. Brittany puppies are amazingly tolerant of children, but young people should be taught to handle her gently. Rough play should never be allowed. When Jill begins to mouth your hands, legs, or furniture, substitute a knotted sock and praise her as she carries it about. Have patience—and remember that puppies do grow up!

For the first few months in your household, Jill will require a great deal of personal attention and time commitment. She is mischievous and likes to play, chew, run, and romp with children or adults. She will grow like a weed, changing from a little ball of puppy fur to a gangly, awkward teenager within a few weeks.

As Jill grows and learns from you, you will learn more and more about her needs. A new puppy adds something special to a family environment, but raising a Brittany puppy isn't a spectator sport. She must learn the rules of the household and you must learn about her character, her likes, dislikes, and the things that satisfy her the most. You can use this knowledge to great advantage when training begins.

Puppy–Proofing Your Home

Don't relax until you have done a hazard inventory of your home and yard. Here are some important things to watch for:

✔ Secure all electrical cords and hanging objects, such as houseplants, well out of your pup's reach.

✔ Latch cabinets to prevent your puppy's investigation and mischief, because household chemicals are extremely dangerous.

=== **TIP** ===

Poison Advice

Don't attempt to treat poisoning on your own unless efforts to obtain professional help fail. Keep in mind that a puppy is quite small and has a rapid metabolic rate, factors that make the danger even greater. Keep these telephone numbers handy: National Poison Center, 800-548-2423 or 900-680-0000; ASPCA Poison Center, 888-426-4435.

✔ Put all chewable objects away or out of reach. That includes children's toys and clothing.

✔ Install special dog gates to prevent your new puppy from falling down stairs and entering rooms where she is not wanted.

✔ If your backyard fence is constructed of wood, it is chewable; thus, make sure that it extends several inches into the ground so Jill can't dig her way out of the yard.

✔ Hang garden hoses out of reach of your venturesome little Brittany, as she may attack and puncture them.

✔ Gardening fertilizers and insecticides present major problems to pups; put all such products well out of your new Brittany's reach to ensure that she doesn't chew on a bag, box, or sprayer hose and ingest toxic chemicals.

✔ When chemicals are applied to the lawn or garden they should be watered well into the soil to prevent Jill from contaminating her feet, then licking the toxins off.

Many household chemicals are quite toxic to Brittany puppies.

Antifreeze and many auto chemicals are highly toxic.

✔ When watering the lawn after the application of chemicals, be sure not to allow Jill to drink from pools or puddles that form on sidewalks. Keep your Brittany off a treated lawn for 48 hours!

✔ If your pup has possibly consumed the contents of dangerous garden products, call your veterinarian immediately. Provide a list of the ingredients on the package label(s) and the amount ingested, if it can be ascertained.

✔ Keep antifreeze out of reach, because many types have sweet tastes that dogs like. Some types contain a kidney toxin that may kill your dog, and unfortunately, treatment is not very effective even when the poisoning is discovered early. If you suspect antifreeze poisoning, seek professional help immediately.

✔ Keep garage doors closed and the driveway free from fluids that may drip from cars.

✔ Virtually all automotive chemicals, including windshield-washer fluid and other alcohol-containing products, are hazardous to Jill's health and must be stored away securely.

✔ Paint, turpentine, thinner, and acetone should be stored well out of the dog's reach. Paint removers are particularly dangerous, and even a quick investigative lick can cause severe tongue burns. A clumsy puppy might tip over a can and soak its feet with the caustic stuff. If that happens, rinse the feet immediately with gallons of cool water. Then wash them off with soap and water and call your veterinarian.

✔ Brittanys are excellent swimmers, but some backyard pools are constructed with escape ladders that only humans can use. If you have such a pool, provide a means of escape for your Brittany before she is allowed to come in contact with the pool. Show her where the steps are, and teach her how to use them.

If the foregoing discussion leaves you with the impression that Brittany puppies are animated, relentless, destructive forces, please understand that these are worst-case scenarios. Brittany puppies are no worse than any other pups, and most Brittany youngsters are not intent on self-destruction. By identifying hazards, you might save your puppy's life.

TIP

A Caveat

A puppy's attraction to an item is directly proportional to the replacement cost of that item.

Exercise

Brittanys thrive on regular exercise. They are athletic sporting dogs that are easily bored if

Look for hazards before exercising your Brittany off-lead in unfamiliar areas.

they have nothing to do. Adequate exercise keeps puppies out of mischief and produces solid musculature in growing youths. Exercise helps to condition adults, keeping them in prime hunting health; it also tends to minimize the effects of aging, such as arthritis. And, obesity can be prevented with exercise and a diet program.

Lack of exercise is rarely a problem when children in the family are available to romp and play with their Brittany companion. However, if Jill is kept indoors or in a kennel run, you are obliged, as her owner, to help her exercise. In a large fenced yard Jill will no doubt initiate and play some games on her own. But don't rely on her self-initiated activity; she needs interactive play sessions, jogging, or regular, frequent long walks to fulfill her exercise requirements. If your lifestyle doesn't allow you to spend time exercising your energetic companion, consider a more sedentary pet.

Minor Behavioral Problems

Chewing

Brittanys are happy, active puppies with active mouths, and like all puppies, they often chew. For some unknown reason, old, worn-out shoes aren't as likely to be chewed as new ones. If allowed, Jill will pass right by a nylon chewy and pick up an expensive shoe. A child's favorite toy or your most expensive gloves are the things that suffer the most abuse.

Chewing is programmed into the makeup of all puppies, but Brittanys are quick learners, and you shouldn't be discouraged from obtaining a young puppy. However, you should realize that your lifestyle will be changed by a new puppy's presence, and you must prepare accordingly. Pick up your personal belongings and stow them out of the pup's reach. Instruct youngsters to pick up their toys and clothes at the same time you are teaching Jill the difference between children's toys and Brittany's toys. Chewing is easily channeled to appropriate objects and is best corrected by substitution. A firm vocal reprimand should accompany each inappropriate chewing episode. Immediately following the reprimand, offer Jill some attractive and appropriate toy such as a nylon bone, knotted sock, or chew stick.

Separation Anxiety

This very serious syndrome is mentioned because the author has received questions from a few Brittany owners, but the condition is not believed to be prevalent among Brittanys. It occurs when Jill is insecure or apprehensive and usually takes place soon after you have gone from home, regardless of the time or reason for your departure. Without warning, she becomes urgently afraid, frets, barks, and sometimes defecates or urinates wherever she happens to be. She may chew up articles that she has never bothered before, such as curtains, tablecloths, books, and any other objects she now notices.

You can possibly stop this anxiety by reducing her concentration on your act of leaving. Here is some advice:

- Depart at varying times of the day.
- Stay away for varying times.
- Leave by a different door.
- Never let her see or hear your car keys.
- Return home without fanfare and act as if you haven't been gone at all.
- Crate her with a cube of dog food (available from pet supply stores), which should occupy her for an hour.

If none of these options is viable, seek help from your veterinarian or a canine behavioral expert.

Automobiles

Few Brittanys suffer fear of riding in cars. If the engine noise or the vehicle's movement frightens Jill, patience and short trips will gradually condition her to those factors.

It is important to make her behave while riding in a car, whether or not she is afraid. Decide where you want Jill to sit and insist that she stay in the designated area. Pet supply stores have dog safety harnesses that fasten into an automobile's seatbelt system and hold the pet in a confined area of the car. If you travel with your Brittany, use a crate if space allows. It is the safest and most positive means of confinement—but please don't put your Brittany in a crate in the car's trunk!

This puppy is checking the newspaper for mischievous new ideas.

Motion sickness is always a messy business; it causes abdominal distress, manifested by nausea, salivation, and vomiting. To guard against this problem, here are some precautions:

- Buy a motion-sickness preventive product from your veterinarian or the pharmacy and give a dose of the drug about two hours before your trip.

Note: Although most such medications are relatively safe, check with your veterinarian about the dosage of any product to factor in considerations such as the dog's size and age.

- Withhold all food and water for two hours before an automobile trip.
- On a long trip, feed Jill small amounts of a high-protein paste supplement. This kind of product is available at most pet supply stores or veterinary offices. It will provide sufficient nutrition without the bulk of regular dog foods.

If you drive a pickup truck, you may be tempted to allow your Brittany to ride in the

Even a well-adjusted Brittany can develop problems when ignored for lengthy periods.

back. Suppress the urge! However, if you can't resist, at least cross-tie Jill so she can't jump from the moving vehicle. Of course, periodically

Choose appropriately sized toys when playing ball with your Brittany pup.

you will need to consult a veterinarian about Jill's eyes, which no doubt will suffer abuse from the dust and debris flying about.

Boarding Kennels

Before you acquire your puppy you should arrange for her care when you can't be home. If you have constructed a kennel run in your backyard, don't expect her to live in it alone. Ask a trustworthy neighbor or friend who knows Jill to care for her in her kennel.

Contact the breeder who raised your puppy, because sometimes breeders have facilities to board your Brittany. If those plans don't work, settle on the least crowded and most secure boarding facility you can find.

Some boarding kennels are spotless and well managed, but unfortunately, many are not. All commercial boarding kennels present stress-related health risks to dogs staying there. Consider these factors:

• Family pets resent being confined to small areas, become bored with inactivity, and become frightened or challenged by the commotion and barking of their kennel mates.

• Diet changes add to the stress of kenneled dogs.

• The odors of females in season are unnerving to intact males.

• A kennel may be a source of fleas, ticks, lice, and other external parasites.

• Inadequate cleaning may predispose boarders to intestinal parasitic infestation.

• The most common complaint resulting from a stay in a boarding facility is "kennel cough," manifested by a chronic, deep, croupy, honking cough that lasts for weeks after the pet returns home.

If you can't avoid boarding Jill in a commercial kennel, visit and tour the facility before you need it. If a tour is denied, you are in the wrong kennel. If you are allowed to walk through the boarding facility, watch for sick animals, signs of diarrhea, vomiting, coughing, and sneezing.

Locate a kennel that specializes in boarding sporting dogs, one in which each dog has its kennel connected to a large outdoor run. The best facilities have runs that are separated from one another by block or brick walls (instead of wire fencing) to minimize conflicts with neighbor dogs and reduce the probability of exposure to respiratory diseases. Responsible boarding kennels require proof of vaccinations prior to boarding your dog.

Identification

Permanent I.D.: Tattoos and Microchips

Even in the best-regulated households, puppies sometimes manage to wander off. Jill should be permanently identified as early as possible by tattooing some identifying numbers or letters on her inner flank or in her ear. Alternatively, you can have a microchip implanted under her skin to provide further identification. Your veterinarian will advise you of the available means of identification and will help implement your choice.

However, no form of protection is effective unless you have the identification registered with an animal relocation program. The AKC maintains a 24-hour hotline service called "Home Again." You register Jill's tattoo or microchip number with that service. The cost is minimal, and your veterinarian, pet supply store, or the AKC can provide you with a regis-

tration form. Veterinarians, shelters, or Brittany rescue organizations can scan for the microchip and look for a flank or ear tattoo. It is the owner's responsibility to notify the Home Again registry of address or phone number changes.

Name Tags

Never allow your Brittany outside without your name and address attached to her. Tags are available through any pet supply shop. Order one with your name, address, and telephone number, and rivet it securely to Jill's collar. Hanging tags may catch on limbs, underbrush, or fences and be pulled off. If nothing better is possible, print your name and telephone number with waterproof ink on the pup's nylon collar. Dogs are commonly lost when their owners are gone from home and they cannot be reached by telephone. If friends are watching your dog while you are on vacation, print their name and phone number in waterproof ink on a piece of gray duct tape and wrap it on Jill's collar.

Permanent identification is critically important for field Brittanys.

Brittanys are natural hunters and most will retrieve from puppyhood without training. However, not all training is so easily accomplished. You must replace some of your Brittany's natural canine behavior with appropriate human-culture conduct. It is natural for a dog to be free of most all restraints, and such tasks as walking on a leash, sitting, or heeling are learned behaviors.

Focus and Rewards

Focus is critical when training. When you have Chip's full attention he is likely to learn what your lesson teaches—and learn it quickly. Schedule all training sessions before his regular meals. If he knows that his reward for success is a tidbit, his focus on you will give him a more willing attitude and greater chance for success. Use treat rewards regularly at first, and later only once in a while, but always reward success with praise and petting.

Collar and Leash Training

Like housebreaking, collar and leash training is a fundamental part of good manners that all dogs should learn. Use a positive approach to teach your Brittany and you will find Chip a

While off-lead, this Brittany is focused on his handler's signals.

willing student. He wants to follow you anyway, and adding a collar and leash doesn't put much stress on his little body and mind. A nylon web collar is available in the correct size and weight at the pet supply store. When buckled on, it should allow two fingers to slide between the collar and his neck.

Introduce Chip to his nylon collar as soon as possible, but for the first two or three days, it shouldn't be left on him when he is alone. Later, when he is no longer troubled by the collar's presence, it is safe to leave it on him all the time, replacing it with a new one when he outgrows it.

Snap a leash about 4 to 6 feet (1.5 to 2 m) long on Chip's collar and let him drag it while you encourage him to move ahead by coaxing and offering him a tidbit now and then. Then pick up the leash and follow him wherever he goes. He will soon connect your presence with the leash, and the leash with reward, and will welcome his leash training each day. It is important to let your Brittany puppy know who is in command and who has control of the leash, but it should be done in a positive way, and never as punishment or correction.

Retractable leashes are lightweight leads of various strengths and lengths that retract into a plastic handle and are available from pet supply stores. They are convenient, offer your dog more freedom than standard leashes, and may be used after Chip has become accustomed to walking on lead, but they should not be used for training.

After Chip accepts his leash (and after he has been vaccinated), you can exercise him outside

his backyard. He will be enthused by the new smells, sights, and sounds and will find them more rewarding than those within his yard. Don't begin obedience training until several weeks later; for a week or two just enjoy the companionship of your new pup.

Advanced Training

Basic obedience training is important if you intend to take Chip on longer walks with you. Begin that training gently, positively, and in short sessions, shortly after he has accepted his leash and knows he is under your control while the leash is in place. Remove the web collar and put on a training collar in its place; snap on a sturdy nylon web leash and begin the first excursion.

Training Collar

A training collar is formed from a short piece of smooth chain or strong nylon fabric with a ring fastened to each end. One size does not fit all dogs! In order to work properly, it should be fitted to the dog and should measure approximately 2 inches (5.1 cm) greater than the circumference of Chip's neck. Most Brittanys respond equally well to either nylon or chain collars.

To form the collar, drop the chain or fabric through one of the rings. Then attach the leash snap to the free ring. Place the collar on the dog so the end of the collar attached to the leash comes up the left side of the dog and crosses from left to right over the top of his neck. Chip is maintained on your left side, and when it's necessary to correct his action, the collar is given a quick tug, then released. If a

A Brittany displaying total focus on its trainer.

training collar is placed on the dog's neck incorrectly, it will not release quickly and may injure him. A training collar that is too long will not close quickly enough to be effective

Pronged collars are constructed of a dozen or so hinged wire prongs; the dull prongs turn against the dog's neck when the leash is tightened. Those collars are banned from the premises of AKC events, are inhumane, and should never be used. If your Brittany is obstreperous or a greater challenge than you can handle with a nylon or chain training collar, try a head halter.

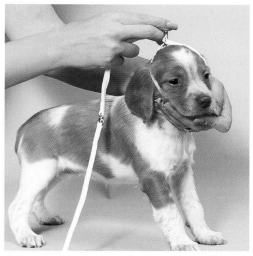

It is never too early to begin collar and leash training.

When you say "*Chip*," you'll get his attention; that lets him know that you are about to give a command that you expect to be followed. After a second or two, give the command and show

Command Clarity

Separate every command into five parts—name, command, action, release, and reward and praise—and make each part clear and distinct. Chip has better hearing than you do, so shouting won't add anything positive to the training. Neither should the command be repeated time and again for a single function.

First, say the dog's name clearly. That is difficult when his name is complex or lengthy, so if necessary, shorten the name and make it simple.

Be sure your Brittany's training collar is put on properly.

Teaching the "come" command using a check leash.

him a treat, but don't reward him until he has performed the command. Then release him (*"Okay!"*) from the command and give him the reward and your praise.

Come

Come is the easiest command to teach your puppy and can be used in many everyday situations and games. You can introduce Chip to *come* at his first feeding time and he won't realize what you are doing. When he is loose in the backyard or in another room, step into his presence, show him his partially full food bowl, and say, "*Chip,*" (hesitation) "*come.*" When he arrives, praise him, put his bowl down, and stand back.

Next, fasten a long lightweight nylon line to Chip's collar and go into the backyard. Allow him to wander away from you for some distance, then drop to one knee and give the command with zeal: "*Chip,*" (hesitation) "*come.*" If Chip doesn't respond immediately, and with the enthusiasm you expect, give a gentle tug on the line to get his attention and repeat the command once. When Chip arrives on your lap, lavish praise on him, then release him from the exercise with an "*Okay,*" give him a tidbit reward, and stand up.

Repeat this exercise frequently at odd times to catch him off guard. When his response to the command has become automatic, try him off leash, but still in the fenced yard. Use it for grooming, feeding, and especially for petting. Never call Chip to you to scold or discipline him or you will defeat your purpose. Regardless of what mischief you have called him away from, each time he comes on command, praise and pet him.

Sit

With Chip standing in front of you, his rump close to a wall, say "*Chip.*" Wait a second, say "*Sit,*" and when that command has been absorbed, hold a tidbit at his eye level, in front of and very close to his muzzle. Move the treat back over his muzzle and skull. He will automatically plunk his bottom on the floor or grass. After sitting for a few seconds, release him with "*Okay,*" praise him, and give him the tidbit.

When Chip doesn't perform the exercise correctly, don't make a big issue of the error; say "*Wrong,*" in a conversational tone. Walk him around the training area for a few minutes and begin again. Practice sitting several times; if you're lucky, he will catch on the very first day, but don't count on it. He may be the smartest Brittany in the world, but don't expect miracles! In the next session, practice the *sit* command several times, and if met with success, progress to another task. If it takes several sessions to learn to *sit* correctly, so be it. You are in no hurry, and some dogs take longer than others to catch on. Ten-week-old puppies have short attention spans, and aren't usually as quick to learn simple exercises as older dogs.

Tip: Reserve the word "*No!*" and a gruff voice for times when Chip is in trouble and you want him to refrain from whatever mischief he is involved in.

Stay

When Chip has mastered *sit* and is looking for his tidbit, instead of saying "*Okay*" and rewarding him, tell him "*Stay*" while you remain standing in front of him. Present your outstretched palm in front of his muzzle as you give the *stay* command. If he begins to lie down or stand up, tell him "*Wrong,*" repeat the command "*Stay,*" and manually put him back into a sitting position. After a few seconds, release him from the *stay* with an "*Okay,*" and give him a reward.

A Brittany being taught to "stay" in the sitting position.

Teaching "down" with a food morsel.

Take only a few backward steps in the beginning. Don't push Chip to the limit and expect him to *stay* interminably the way well-trained dogs in obedience trials do. Return quickly to his side, take your position with him on your left, pick up his leash, and release him from the *stay* command. Most puppies are doing well if they stay for 20 seconds without fidgeting.

Down

This command is used in obedience trials, and is also a convenient way to let Chip relax while you talk to neighbors. It should be given in the same way the *sit* command is used. Begin the exercise with the dog in the sitting or standing position, his rump against a wall. "*Chip*," (hesitation), "*down*," is the command. Don't confuse him by using extra words. Never tell him "*Lie down*" or confound him even more by saying "*Chip, come here and lie down.*"

After you have given the *down* command, hold a tidbit on the floor between his forelegs, near his sternum so low and close that he can't reach it without lying down and inching backward.

After the *down* command, tell him to *stay*, then back away a few steps. Finish the exercise by returning to him, releasing him from the exercise, rewarding and lauding great praise upon him. Once Chip realizes that you aren't really leaving him, and if he stays you will return with more praise and tidbits, he will be happy to cooperate.

Off

This is another logical and valuable command for Chip to learn. It tells your pup to stop what he is doing and place all four feet on the ground. *Off* means to get off the furniture, to get his feet off the windowsill, to stop jumping on a

Consistency is important. Always use the same technique and break the command into several parts. First, his name, then the command, then the action, the release, and finally, the reward and praise.

The next step is to back away from Chip while he is obeying the *stay* command. When you put the leash on the ground and start to move away, your faithful Brittany will try to follow. Say "*Wrong*," repeat the *stay* command, manually place Chip in the sitting position, display your outstretched flat palm, and back away again. After a few tries, the pup will get the idea and stay put while you take several steps backward; then you must return to his side to finish the exercise. Don't forget to release him from the *stay*, and never finish the exercise without reward and praise.

A yummy treat holds this Brittany's focus.

person, another dog, or any other object. It is taught in much the same way as any other command, except that you must wait until an appropriate moment to use the command to make the lesson meaningful. When he puts his feet on the floor, tell him *"Okay,"* offer him a tidbit reward and your praise, and he won't forget it.

Heel

Each time you bring out Chip's leash, he realizes that a training session or a walk is on the morning's agenda, either of which is an opportunity to receive a yummy tidbit.

Heeling is an exercise that all prospective obedience competitors should learn. Place Chip on your left side, running the leash through your left hand and holding it with your right. Give him the crisp command, *"Chip, sit."* Then as you step off with your left foot, give the command *"Heel"* and give the leash a little tug. As you walk forward, use his leash to keep him walking with his nose by your left knee. If Chip tries to lag behind, encourage him to keep up with you by teasing him along with a tidbit held in your right hand. Soon he will be walking by your side, taking turns and stops in his stride.

This is a tough exercise for an ambitious puppy to master. Chip is eager to forge ahead and investigate something at the far end of his leash. Keep the slack out of the leash, but don't

═══ TIP ═══

Heeling

Heeling is fine for obedience trials, or for maximum control of your dog in a crowd. Under those special circumstances it is important, but that's where heeling should end. Heeling is boring for Chip and he should be given more freedom whenever the situation will allow.

hold it too tightly. At first, leave enough slack for him to move a step ahead of or behind you, but don't allow him to bolt ahead or stop. If he moves past your left knee, repeat the command *heel*, and quickly pivot to your right and proceed in the opposite direction. Soon Chip will

A Brittany on point while being trained with check cord.

watch where you put your left foot and keep his body in line with your leg.

After he has properly *heeled* for a dozen steps, stop, tell him to *sit*, release him with an "*Okay*," and reward him with a tidbit and praise. Play for a minute or two, and begin the exercise all over again.

Leashes and collars are Chip's apparel. His web collar is his everyday wear, while his chain or nylon training collar tells Chip that you intend to maintain maximum control and he will expect training or a sojourn out of the yard. The retractable leash and web collar mean a romp in the dog park.

Teacher's Instructions

Love your student! All puppies, but especially Brittanys, are active, inquisitive, and energetic, and they sometimes misbehave.

• Don't make a federal case out of Chip's mistake. It is natural for him to play and have fun. Don't lose your sense of humor, and as his teacher, you should always try to make his education as enjoyable as possible.

• No training session should last more than five minutes. If continued for too long, he will become bored and lose interest.

• Change frequently from one task to another.

• Don't forget to play with Chip between lessons, and always end training sessions with playtime.

• Take your time; what he doesn't learn today he will learn tomorrow.

• Reward amply and in timely fashion but don't overdo the treats.

• Don't expect him to be ready for an obedience trial at the end of the first month.

• Never use negative reinforcement. Don't scold or grouch at your Brittany for being

This Brittany is "honoring" or backing a point struck by a fellow hunter, a pointer.

guilty of nothing more than bouncing up when he should be sitting. Corporal punishment is out! Chip will remember every swat you dole out, but he won't remember why it was administered. Hitting or scolding will teach him only one thing: that you sometimes, for no reason, go insane and hurt him.

In order to fix the learned behavior in his mind and make it automatic, training must be continually repeated. Repeat each learned task once every day, or if that isn't possible, repeat each one several times a week. And above all, remember that playing is natural but sitting, staying, and heeling are learned behaviors.

HOW-TO: HOUSEBREAK

Getting Started

Brittanys are naturally clean dogs and many will house-break themselves if given ample opportunity to do so. It is the nature of all wolves and dogs to avoid soiling their living space. To teach Chip to use a certain area of the yard is simply expanding on his natural tendencies to separate his eliminations from his den. All companion dogs and gun-dogs should be housebroken even if your Brittany lives outside most of the time, because you might want to travel—and a dog that is not housebroken is not apt to be a welcome guest anywhere.

Young puppies use little discretion; when they feel the urge to urinate or defecate, they just do it and the job is finished before you notice—but then it's too late to correct. A professional dog trainer has estimated that to be effective, your response to Chip's "accident" must occur within five seconds from the time it happens. Beyond that amount of time, he will not associate his defecating or urinating action with any corrective measure you may take. He won't connect being chastised with his natural act, but he will remember that you suddenly lost your cool, berated him, and scolded him, for no apparent reason! To an untrained pup, urinating or defecating isn't a mistake or an accident; it's natural and is done automatically, without thought or planning.

Don't use a negative approach to housebreaking. A pup has no way of knowing about human customs or habits until he is taught. It is a serious error to punish, scold, or reprimand a puppy for messing on the floor. Rubbing his nose in his urine is equally confusing to the pup and isn't likely to make a lasting, positive impression on him. Once the act of urination or defecation is completed, it's gone from his mind.

Tip: Always remember the five-second rule.

Step by Step

✔ On his first day in your home, immediately take Chip from your car to an area of the backyard, perhaps behind a hedge or in an old garden spot. The toilet area should be off the beaten path and should not be cleaned up for several days to allow the odors of his urine and feces to be established there.

✔ Take Chip to the same designated area of the yard frequently, and soon he will seek out that spot whenever he gets the urge to go.

✔ Take him to the toilet area immediately after each meal, when he wakes in the morning, after naps, before bedtime at night, and anytime he fusses during the night. If you are able to train yourself to that task, your Brittany pup will be housebroken before you know it.

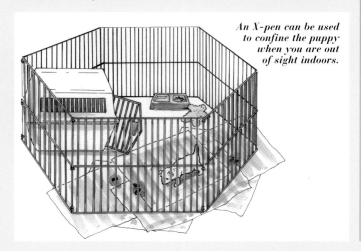

An X-pen can be used to confine the puppy when you are out of sight indoors.

✔ For the first week or so, don't let Chip out of your sight when he is indoors.

✔ Each time he squats to urinate or defecate, say "*No*" in a normal tone, pick him up, and carry him to the toilet area in the yard. Even if he has started to urinate or defecate, he should be carried to the toilet area to finish. Don't let him finish on the floor and *then* take him outside; that will only train Chip to take a trip to the backyard after his elimination.

✔ After he has emptied his bladder or bowel in the toilet area, praise him, play with him for a moment, and allow him back inside.

Reliable Tools

Prevention, substitution, and positive reinforcement are the most reliable tools to use in housebreaking your pup.

✔ *Prevent* him from messing on the floor by confining him to a pen or crate; never let him out of your sight while in the house.

✔ *Substitute* the toilet area of the yard for your carpet. When Chip shows signs of turning in circles in preparation for eliminating his bowel, pick him up quickly and get him to the toilet area.

✔ *Praise and reward* him when he complies and deposits his eliminations in the appropriate place. Great patience is required to housebreak a pup, but persistence will pay off.

Tip: Try attaching a bell on a string on the inside of the back door. Most 12-week-old Brittany pups will learn to ring the bell to go outside with minimal training. To teach Chip to use the bell, take him to the door, hold his foot in your hand, ring the bell, then open the door and call or lead him to the toilet area.

Nighttime Training

✔ During Chip's housebreaking, pick up his food and water at least two hours before bedtime.

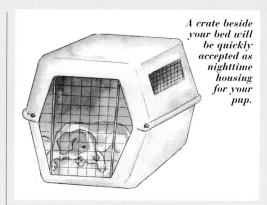

A crate beside your bed will be quickly accepted as nighttime housing for your pup.

✔ Confine him in his crate or a small pen beside your bed.

✔ Each time he fusses, get out of bed and carry him to his toilet area. Wait a few minutes, then pick him up and return him to his crate.

✔ A fundamental concept of training is that Chip's nighttime fussing means a trip to the toilet. It doesn't mean attention, playtime, or food.

Tip: Don't try to reason with a nine-week-old puppy. Brittanys are intelligent dogs, but their reasoning powers are not easily engaged at an early age.

Paper-Training

Paper-training isn't recommended except in peculiar situations. If you must leave Chip inside the house by himself for extended periods, teaching him to use newspapers for a toilet might be warranted. If you find it necessary to paper-train him, buy an X-pen and confine him to it all the time you aren't with him. Cover half the floor of the pen with a dozen thicknesses of newspaper, and set his food and water dishes, bed, and toys in the other half. Chip will use the paper-covered area for eliminations right away. Always clean up his messes as soon as you see them.

FEEDING YOUR BRITTANY

A discussion of canine nutrition should begin with one simple fact. If something sounds too good to be true, it probably is. A dog food that costs pennies per pound is worth about what you pay for it, because no one can produce dollars' worth of nutrition and sell it for a few cents. A Brittany's appearance, energy, and stamina are directly related to the quantity and quality of its food.

Types of Foods Available

Three types of dog foods are currently on the market: canned, semimoist, and dry. Many companies produce all three.

Canned Foods

Canned foods are expensive, but they store well and are highly palatable. However, feeding canned food alone may not give Jill an adequate amount of roughage in her diet. Canned food is more than 60 percent water and has preservatives that may cause a diuretic (urinary frequency) effect when fed exclusively. Furthermore, the meat contained in canned dog foods often isn't of the highest quality in spite of what dog food commercials would have you believe.

Good nutrition must be continued from puppyhood throughout life.

Semimoist Foods

Semimoist or soft-moist foods that are marketed in sealed see-through packets also are quite palatable, but they don't store as well as canned foods. They look like hamburger or other ground meat and sell well because of their appearance. They are generally more expensive and contain rather large amounts of sugar and some chemical preservatives that are not found in dry foods. Increased water consumption often accompanies their use, resulting in frequent urination. Semimoist foods are also occasionally blamed for allergic reactions.

Dry Foods

Dry dog foods are usually the least expensive and easiest to feed. Balanced nutrition is possible for a Brittany using dry food exclusively. However, all dry foods are not the same. They

===== TIP =====

Turnover

Regardless of the food you choose, always note its turnover or popularity before you purchase it. Ask the store's department manager which food is restocked most frequently, then read the label on the package carefully and check the ingredients before making your purchase.

vary greatly in nutritional content and palatability. You shouldn't need to flavor a dry food to get a healthy dog to eat it and you shouldn't need to add supplements to a dry dog food to make it complete and balanced.

Quantity: Dry dog food should be bought in quantities that correspond to the size and number of dogs you are feeding. How much can one Brittany puppy eat? It is true that dog food is less expensive in 50-pound bags, but unless it is used up quickly, storage will take its toll on nutrients. Fats may become rancid; vitamins A, D, E, K, and some B complex may be lost. For that same reason, beware of buying Jill's food from stores that have a low product turnover.

Storage: Dry dog food should be kept in an airtight container. Preservatives and additives protect the food from oxidation and also maintain the palatability of dry foods. Some foods contain no chemical preservatives and are protected with natural antioxidants such as vitamins C and E. Look for those foods, because they are often the best. Don't store dry dog food in a warm place; higher temperatures enhance deterioration of the ingredients.

Categories of Dry Food

We arbitrarily divide dry dog foods into three general categories: premium, commercial, and generic.

Premium brands are usually the most expensive dry dog foods. They are sold in veterinary hospitals, pet supply stores, and supermarkets, and most of them are well accepted by Brittanys. Premium dry dog foods contain adequate nutrition, require no supplementation, and are sufficiently tasty to suit even the most finicky appetites. In many cases, premium dry foods may be fed free choice, meaning that the food is left out so your Brittany has access to it at all times. Naturally that is not an option if Jill is overweight. If Jill is a finicky eater you can mix her premium dry food with a small amount of a premium canned food.

Commercial brands are those dry dog foods that are found stacked on the shelves of grocery supermarkets and discount department stores. Many of those products provide excellent nutrition, and some brands have held their place in the market for decades. That is an indication that they provide adequate nutrition for the average canine pet, although they vary greatly in quality. To be sure that your selection is correct, contact the manufacturer and ask for the data on the food being considered. You should receive a report on feeding trials being conducted, the sources of all the ingredients, and the nutritional analysis.

Generic brands always should be considered when shopping. However, a major problem with generic foods is that they may vary in composition from month to month, depending on the availability and cost of their ingredients. Generic foods are rarely subjected to feeding trials because of the expense of those trials.

This happy trio of Brittanys enjoy excellent nutrition.

Dog Food Labels

Pass up any dog food that doesn't plainly list its composition. Dog foods containing the best ingredients and balanced nutritional elements will proudly display that information. Know what you are feeding Jill! Don't buy a dog food because it is low in price or because the total protein is higher than in other brands, and don't choose a food by the picture on a bag. The *sources* and *quality* of protein, carbohydrate, and fat are as important as the quantities.

Don't base your selection on television ads. Those ads typically show a beautiful litter of puppies, a happy companion dog, or a group of "winning" dogs. Those paid actors are marketing tools, and they may or may not promote a superior dog food.

Labels may state that the dog food meets the recommendations of the National Research Council (NRC). That statement applies only to canine *maintenance* requirements, meaning that the food should be adequate for pets under minimal stress. However, for growing puppies, competition dogs, or dogs in heavy training, maintenance foods may not be acceptable, because they don't supply the necessary energy demands.

Labels may specify the quantities of available nutrients, instead of the quantities of *bioavailable* nutrients, which is the amount of the food a dog can actually use for its energy requirements. If an essential element is fed in a form that is not bioavailable, it might as well be left on the store shelf.

Look for the source of protein. The ingredient list should give you that information. Vegetable protein sources such as corn or soy flour may provide an excellent analysis on the package,

A weekend hunter with his well-fed Brittany.

can be assured that products so labeled contain the right amount of bioavailable food elements required for puppies, youths, and adults.

Tip: If the AAFCO declaration is not shown, get a phone number from the package and call the manufacturer. Obtain feeding trial results. Ask about the sources of protein and fat. Request information about the formulation of the products, and ask if the formula is kept constant, regardless of seasonal variations of ingredient costs.

Be picky! If you can't find the desired information about a product, choose another brand. If you are unable to understand information provided by manufacturers, consult your veterinarian. If she or he isn't able to help you make the decision, borrow a text on the subject or look it up on the Internet. Most veterinary clinics have reference sources for nutritional requirements of dogs.

Nutritional Elements

Water

Fresh drinking water is critical. Other nutritional elements may be varied under different circumstances, but a source of clean water is always essential. That doesn't mean adding clean water to a dirty bowl. Like you, Jill prefers fresh, cool water in a clean bowl.

Protein

Protein (or its components, known as amino acids) comes from animal or vegetable sources. Vegetable amino acids have lower bioavailability than those derived from animal proteins.

but it may be misleading if that protein is not bioavailable.

Caution: All dog foods are not equal. Read package labels and call or write to manufacturers.

Feeding Trials

You will find foods with label declarations that have passed the American Association of Feed Control Officials (AAFCO) feeding trials for the entire life cycle of canines. Generally you

Modern dogs are carnivores by definition, but in practice are omnivores (eat both meat and vegetables). Most prefer the flavor and texture of meat, which is natural, considering canine genetic background. Plant protein is less palatable to your Brittany.

Fat

Fat is a part of all balanced diets. Fat of either animal or plant origin is a calorie-dense nutrient that contains 9 Kcal (the amount of heat energy required to raise 2.2 pounds—1 kg—of water from 15 to 16 degrees C) per gram. That is more than twice the calories contained in protein or carbohydrates. Palatability is the principal difference between vegetable oils and animal fats; both provide adequate fatty acids.

Carbohydrates

Carbohydrates, or starches, are derived from vegetables. For the human, carbohydrates are important as the principal sources of glucose, but dogs don't require them. However, carbohydrates provide calories, and it is impractical to produce dog food commercially without them. Dog foods that are high in carbohydrates and contain protein and fat derived only from plant sources are not recommended. The best nutrition for Jill is a food that combines animal protein with carbohydrates and fats.

Supplements

Coat or growth supplements are available but they may endanger your dog's nutritional balance and are usually unnecessary. Everyone wants his or her Brittany's coat to be shiny with rich colors, but the best way to ensure that appearance is through good nutrition, not from a bottle of coat enhancer. Obtain a veterinarian's advice before you use vitamin and mineral supplements or coat enhancers like lecithin, vitamin A, and fatty acid preparations.

Caution: Don't feed Jill a bargain brand of dog food and hope to cover its deficiencies with a cheap vitamin-mineral supplement. Considering the time and expense you have spent on your Brittany, dog food is a poor place to economize.

If you wish to read about the intricacies of canine nutrition, purchase a book by the National Research Council called *Nutrient Requirements of Dogs* (revised edition). It is updated regularly and will answer virtually all of your technical questions about canine nutrition.

Chew Sticks and Treats

Rawhide bones, cartilage from pigs' ears, cattle hooves, and nylon bones have been available for many years and millions of them have been chewed by dogs of all sizes and breeds. However, recent papers by canine experts report that animal-origin chewies in all forms are dangerous and that rawhide chewies have caused many cases of intestinal blockage. The author is personally unaware of any such problems with those products, but you should ask Jill's veterinarian before you buy them.

Dog biscuits or treats are available in various forms and sizes and are harmless unless they are used as principal sources of nutrition. They are not part of a balanced diet, and should be used only when you wish to reward Jill or give her something to do. They are excellent treats to use when you put her in her crate or leave her in her run for a while.

Soft treats, such as bits of liver or other meat, should be reserved for training rewards, and should not be fed in large quantities.

A beautiful Brittany displaying the form and fitness of being in excellent condition.

Sharp splinters from the bones may lodge in the dog's mouth or throat, or the splinters may be swallowed, where they can cause other problems.
• Junk food such as ice cream, candy, pizza, potato chips, and a host of other snacks are difficult for the dog to digest, will upset her nutritional balance, and should be avoided.

Frequency of Feeding

Post-weaning, puppies should be fed four times a day with free choice dry food plus two moist meals of mixed canned and dry food. That feeding program should be continued until Jill is six months of age. From six months until she is one year old, feed her three meals daily, or if free choice dry food is continued, give her one moist meal per day. At a year of age, most Brittanys will thrive on two meals a day or free choice dry food alone.

An exception to this feeding schedule applies to gluttonous eaters or multiple-dog households where dogs compete for the food. Another exception is the dog with a finicky appetite (a rare occurrence in Brittanys). If Jill is a finicky eater, the meals of canned food mixed with dry may be continued indefinitely.

Nutritional Problems

Obesity is too common in Brittanys. Fat dogs aren't healthy, and if Jill is a gluttonous eater you must feed her accordingly.
• Feed measured amounts, weigh her regularly, and adjust her meals according to her weight.
• Separate her from other dogs at mealtime.

Homemade Diets

Diets that are formulated in the family kitchen often lead to problems. Leave dog food production to those companies that have laboratories, research facilities, and colonies of dogs for feeding trials to prove the value of their products.

Dietary No-No's

• Don't feed Jill milk of any kind, because it will usually cause diarrhea.
• Organ meats like liver, heart, or kidney often cause diarrhea.
• Highly seasoned foods usually will cause stomach upsets.
• Table scraps may upset her stomach and definitely will interfere with her nutritional balance.
• Cooked bones of any origin or size are dangerous to give your Brittany. Chicken or chop bones, steak bones, and some roast bones may splinter when the dog chomps down on them.

This Brittany needs good nutrition to support its hard work at water retrieving.

A Brittany retrieving the family's dinner entrée.

• Substitute a portion of her regular food with a low-calorie filler such as ground carrots or canned green beans. An option is a special low-calorie dog food diet if that is easier for you.

• Older dogs often are lazy and may become obese. As Jill ages and begins to exercise less, reevaluate her nutritional needs. Consult your veterinarian about feeding her smaller quantities of a higher-quality food.

• Dogs that gain weight and develop a voracious appetite should be examined by a veterinarian, because a number of health problems, including diabetes, may cause obesity.

Caution: Be sure to increase your dog's nutritional intake if she is undergoing training or when bird season rolls around.

Skinny Brittanys are often impossible to put weight on because they are so ambitious and energetic that they burn all the calories they consume. Feed such Brittanys premium foods, free choice, with a meal or two of dry food mixed with canned food each day. If you notice weight loss or decreased energy in your normally active and athletic Brittany, take her to your veterinarian.

Food and Water Bowls

Buy stainless steel bowls for Jill's food and water. Glass bowls usually don't last long. Fired-clay bowls may contain toxins in the paint. Aluminum or plastic bowls are porous and may house bacteria. Invest in a pair of heavy stainless steel bowls large enough to hold Jill's food when she is an adult. Purchase a rack for the bowls that keeps them upright and anchors them in place.

If free choice feeding is a part of your dog's nutritional program, wash and fill the food bowl daily. Don't buy a large self-feeder, or if one is used, be sure to clean it regularly and inspect it frequently for bugs.

GROOMING YOUR BRITTANY

Grooming means more than combing and brushing. It includes a brief physical checkup and should be done at least weekly, and usually more often. Chip's coat reflects his nutritional status and physical condition. Frequent grooming sessions may reveal problems before signs and symptoms begin.

There are many factors that can influence coat quality:
- Nutritional status can be determined by feeling the fatty cover over his ribs.
- External parasite infestations may rob Chip of nutrition and cause his coat to deteriorate.
- Estrus (heat) periods will usually cause a female to lose coat quantity and quality.
- Stress of injury or illness always affects your Brittany's coat.
- Seasonal, twice yearly, shedding necessitates additional grooming.
- As Chip ages, his coat will dry as his nutritional needs change and will require reevaluation.

Regular grooming produces a happy companion.

Grooming is a major consideration for Brittany owners. Even if Chip's coat is shiny and has a natural sheen, you aren't relieved of your grooming responsibilities. Routine grooming procedures should be scheduled, and not left to "when I find time." An equally bad plan is to delegate the dog's grooming duties to an uninformed individual.

When to Groom and Why

Grooming Chip is an important part of bonding and training and should begin shortly after you acquire him. The time you spend grooming him serves multiple purposes.

1. As you groom you examine him and may uncover some minor skin problem before it has become serious.

Brittanys require an abundance of handling that usually begins with grooming.

for minor pad abrasions and lacerations. And keep an eye out for skin tumors and fleas, ticks, and other external parasites before they become a serious problem.

Coat Care

Combing

Comb thoroughly. When you encounter mats, use a mat splitter or a pair of blunt pointed scissors to cut them out, but take care not to nick Chip's ear leathers or the web between his toes. Also, pay particular attention to the area of his back in front of his tail. After the initial combing and brushing, run a fine-tooth flea comb through the hair of that area. If fleas are present, they will hop out ahead of the comb or will be caught in its teeth. Don't forget to reward Chip when he stands quietly, and don't be cross if he is impatient and eager for you to finish.

Toenail, Ear, Eye, and Tooth Care

Toenails

Trim Chip's nails using a sharp nail trimmer of the scissors type. Never use a dull instrument. Long, pointed puppy nails may need weekly trimming. For active outdoor Brittanys, the nails of the forefeet require trimming only when you hear them pecking on the floor. Hind nails suffer less wear than the front ones because they aren't used in digging; but they should be checked on a regular basis. Old dogs'

2. Bonding occurs every time you spend personal time with your Brittany.

3. Grooming is training, because your puppy is taught to stand or sit still on the table while you groom and examine him. In fact, leadership training begins on the grooming table.

4. Chip will look beautiful and you will feel better after a grooming session.

Grooming is serious business and not playtime. Place Chip on a table covered with a rug or towel held in place with picnic-table clips. Curtail his wriggling and desire to jump while you're combing him and remember that he respects the person who handles him and with whom he spends the most time. Each time you groom Chip, you are reestablishing yourself as his alpha pack leader.

After Chip has grown up and taken to the hunting field, grooming becomes more important. Look for thistles and cheat-grass awns between his toes and tangled in his coat. Check

Nail trimming is an integral part of routine grooming.

nails should be checked more often than those of younger animals.

Most Brittany's toenails are light colored, and usually at least a few are sufficiently transparent for you to see the blood vessels forming a point in the core of the nail. That point is termed the *quick*, which you should identify because the quick also contains sensory nerves. Your first cut should be just outside the quick. By visually noting the length of the white nail after trimming it, you should have a good idea about how much to take off the darker nails. If in doubt, begin cutting off thin, serial slices of the nail, starting at the tip. As you progress, you will discover that the nail becomes softer with each slice. Near the tip of the nails, the cross-sections of the slices will be hollow at the bottom, an inverted V shape. As you near the blood vessels, the slices will become more nearly circular when viewed in cross-section.

Slight bleeding from a nail isn't cause for alarm. Toenail bleeding isn't likely to be profuse, but it may be persistent. To stop the bleeding, press a dampened styptic shaving stick firmly to the bleeding nail, hold it in place for several minutes, and keep Chip confined to his crate for an hour after stopping the bleeding.

Tip: Several blood-stopping products that work as well as a styptic stick are available from pet supply stores, including powders and liquids.

Ears

Examine Chip's ears each time he is groomed and after each trip to the field, whether hunting or just walking in the woods. Ear cleaning is an important part of regular grooming in hunt-ing dogs. If you notice a significant amount of wax or dirt in the outer ear canal, it is easily cleaned with a cotton ball that has been slightly moistened with hydrogen peroxide. Never pour a cleaning solution into Chip's ears unless advised to do so by your veterinarian. When you are inspecting his ears, be aware of unusual sensitivity. Hold the ear flap up, and look into the canal if he scratches at either or

Never use a cotton applicator stick in your Brittany's ear! Instead, clean with a cotton ball moistened with hydrogen peroxide.

A Brittany's eyes should be checked daily and cleaned when needed.

both ears or holds his head tipped to the side. If you see a foreign object that can be reached easily, pluck it out with hemostat forceps. If you can't see the object, or if the ear canal has excessive wax, or if the dog continues to tip his

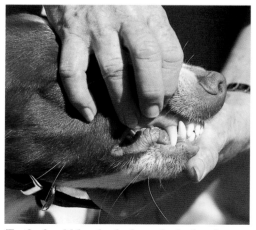

Teeth should be checked regularly for the beginning of tartar deposits.

head, have him examined by your veterinarian. Grass awns are commonly found in the outer ear canals of field dogs, and may migrate deep in the canal and cause a serious infection.

Eyes

Inspect Chip's eyes after each time he runs in the field, as well as when he is groomed. Look for redness, irritation, and foreign objects. A grass seed that is trapped under an eyelid will cause the dog to squint. Use copious amounts of tepid water or eyewash to try to wash it out—but do not rub his eye or attempt to remove the object with tweezers or forceps. It is easier (and cheaper) to have the foreign material removed by Chip's veterinarian before it has rubbed on the cornea and created a corneal ulcer that must also be treated.

Teeth

Open Chip's mouth and examine his teeth for abnormalities. If you notice a soft yellow plaque or tartar, it is time to begin brushing Chip's teeth. An easy way to remove the soft tartar is with a finger wrapped in gauze soaked with hydrogen peroxide. Don't try to hold his mouth open; instead, slip your gauze-covered finger inside the lips and rub it across the outside surface of his teeth. Another option is to use specially flavored canine toothpaste and either a canine toothbrush or a rubber finger brush that slides over your index finger. Squeeze a short ribbon of canine toothpaste on the brush, slide it under the dog's lips, and rub the outside surface of his teeth. It takes only a couple of minutes and he won't object to the procedure, because the canine toothpaste has a pleasant taste.

If Chip is given rawhide or nylon bones to chew and is fed primarily dry dog food, his

A water-retrieving Brittany standing in the river, waiting for action.

teeth shouldn't require much routine care. Older Brittanys, those that are always fed soft food, and those that don't chew a lot may be subject to tartar deposits if their teeth aren't brushed regularly. As the tartar builds up, it invades and erodes the gums and causes bacterial infections that, if allowed to progress unchecked, will eventually cause the teeth to loosen. Chronic gum infection may predispose older dogs to arthritis and heart and kidney disease. If tartar builds up in spite of your efforts, your veterinarian can scale the teeth with ultrasonic equipment and dental instruments. That procedure may require a short-acting general anesthetic.

Bathing

• Bathe Chip if his coat is deeply soiled, fouled, or shortly before a dog show.
• When he encounters a skunk or finds something particularly rancid to roll in along the hiking trail, it's time for a bath.

• Baths also help finalize semiannual seasonal shedding.

When bathing is deemed necessary, squeeze a small amount of petroleum jelly in each of the dog's eyes and place a stretched and twisted cotton ball in each ear. Place Chip on a mat in the bathtub and soak his coat thoroughly with warm water using a spray nozzle, holding it close to his skin. Use small amounts of a non-insecticide dog shampoo (with pH of 7.5) and work it into a good lather. Keep the soap well away from his face and eyes and don't squirt water into his face. When satisfied that the entire coat has been lathered, hold the spray nozzle close to his skin and work it around to rinse the soap from his coat, going over his body several times until all shampoo is gone.

Towel Chip several times, rubbing his coat vigorously and changing towels frequently to squeeze as much water as possible from his coat. Take him out of the bathtub and, using the warm setting on a handheld hair dryer, complete the drying procedure.

The intelligent and biddable Brittany often does well in obedience trials, field trial competition, and hunting trials. They hold their own in tracking trials, are competitive in agility, and might be seen in freestyle obedience (dancing). Their medium size, ease of care, and desirable temperament make the multipurpose Brittany an ideal hunter, companion, playmate, and show dog.

Companion Dog

American dogs rarely work in the jobs for which they were originally bred. Most dogs serve multiple functions, the most vital of which is to bring refreshing interludes into the lives of their human consorts. They are our pals, our friends, and they play extremely important roles in our lives. For the most part, Americans are responsible dog owners. We love, feed, and care for our dogs at our own expense and are willing to sacrifice a portion of our precious time and hard earned money just to enjoy their beneficial, loyal, and amicable presence. Companion dogs add years to our lives and earn their living by being agreeable

A beautiful Brittany show dog standing ready for inspection.

cohorts. The principal job for Brittanys in America is being a "companion dog."

Hunter and Retriever

Pointing and retrieving are natural to most Brittanys. However, many people acquire Brittanys merely for private weekend shooting expeditions, with no intention of training them for field competition and using them only to assist in putting grouse, quail, pheasants, or other game birds on the table for Sunday dinner.

There is no single correct way to train a dog for any discipline, including hunting or retrieving. In this case, the training method depends on your knowledge, experience, and willingness—yours and your dog's—to learn what's involved.

Gundog training by a professional trainer is sometimes necessary.

Jill is trainable and has inherent talents that should help you tackle the tasks at hand. It will help if you have previously hunted with a bird dog, seen Brittanys perform, and can recognize your limitations. Obtain advice from an experienced gundog trainer, buy a book, follow directions, and join a club. But don't *ever* take a chance of spoiling a fine Brittany because of your own lack of knowledge or ability to care for her.

Tip: For the average weekend hunter, training your own dog can be fun and rewarding. Patience is critical to success. If you see that your efforts are failing, ask for help but don't give up!

Formal retriever training, field trial training, and gundog training are beyond the scope of this manual, but some hints are offered to help you start your Brittany.

• Begin training when Jill is very young, but if she doesn't catch on quickly, wait a week and try again.

• Train before meals.

• Keep each training session short—about ten minutes.

• Don't repeat any lesson so frequently that she loses interest in it.

• Be consistent; training should be undertaken by one instructor, using only one technique.

• Simple obedience commands (*come, sit, stay*) must be mastered before Jill can begin gundog training.

• Use a canvas or feathered dummy or a fabric-covered lightweight object, such as a tennis ball tied in a sock.

• Squeeze a few drops of bird scent on the dummy being used. Bird scents are available at sporting goods stores; in a pinch, you can rub a hotdog on the dummy.

Tip: Hard or heavy objects such as sticks, bones, hard rubber balls, or golf balls should never be used to train a retriever because they can promote development of a hard mouth.

• Attach a long, lightweight nylon cord to Jill's web collar.

• Take a firm grip on her collar and tell her "*Sit.*"

• Get her attention by letting her smell the dummy.

• Toss the dummy in a high arc directly in front of her, and while it is in the air, tell her "*Mark.*"

• When she sees where the dummy has landed, say "*Jill, fetch,*" and let go of the collar.

• After she has picked up the dummy, kneel down and tell her "*Jill, come*"; keep her cord snug but don't tug or pull. She will probably run to you.

• When she reaches you, stand, hold out your hand, and tell her "Give," and with your other hand, offer her a tidbit, which she can't take unless she releases the dummy. When you have received the dummy, release her ("*Okay*"),

Retriever training for this three-month-old Brittany pays off.

reward her with *"Good dog,"* and give her the treat. Don't play tug-of-war. If she drops the dummy on the ground, walk to where it has fallen, pick it up, hold it before her, and when she accepts it, proceed back to where you were.
• Repeat this exercise a few times daily until you and she are comfortable with her performance, then remove the cord and continue to polish her retrieving.

In the beginning it is important to give Jill a reward after each successful retrieve. This reinforces her retriever instinct, and elicits better cooperation when she is taken to the field. After a few sessions, most of the time a pat on the head and *"Good dog"* takes the place of the reward.

Seeking and Pointing

Obtain a scented game-bird wing. Keep it in a tightly closed plastic bag, and when Jill is in the car or house, hide the wing in tall grass. (A pigeon or dove wing with a couple of drops of game-bird scent is fine.) Attach your long line to Jill's collar and walk in the general area where you have hidden the wing. When she smells it, watch her closely. When she points the wing, speak to her quietly, letting her know she is doing what you want. If she tries to rush ahead, steady her with the cord, speaking to her all the time. Your voice and action will let her know that this is an important smell to remember.

Tip: A scented bird wing will keep best in a plastic bag in your freezer when not in use.

Flash Point

Take Jill to a nearby field or meadow where birds abound. They need not be game birds in the beginning. You will probably see your puppy assume an instinctive pointing stance for a split second when she perceives the presence

Check-line training for "whoa" command.

of a bird under cover. This pause is termed a *flash point,* and is to be encouraged. When you have recognized the flash point repeatedly, it is time to teach her to hold the point.

Quietly tell Jill *"Whoa"* as you move to her side while she assumes the pointing stance. Then with gentle hands and voice, encourage her to remain steady on point. You can then send her to flush the bird. The *whoa* command is very important for a field dog to master. If she always pauses when she hears *whoa,* your tone of voice can change to make her hold the flash point, or to stop suddenly in her tracks.

Place a scented bird wing on the end of a fishing line and hide it in the grass. When she has stopped and has held her flash point for a second, hold her gently with the check line and, with your fishing pole, release the bird wing (jerk it in the air). Tell Jill *"Whoa"* to teach her to stand still when birds fly away. This command will teach her not to chase birds that land and fly away in your yard.

Note: A well-trained dog will point birds, not chase them.

Guns

A cap pistol or .22 caliber gun loaded with blanks is often used in early gundog training. Later, after the dog has become accustomed to the noise, a shotgun can be used. The object is to correlate the noise of the gun with marking and fetching the training dummy. Always fire the gun in front of your Brittany so that the concussion and noise will be directed away from her. Never fire a gun close to her head. Jill's sense of hearing is extremely sensitive and must always be protected.

She should soon master backyard fetching, and her instinct to point birds under cover will become as natural as her name. At this time, she is probably ready for her first expedition into the field. Be patient. Don't expect a miracle. In the beginning, keep your long checkline on Jill's collar to hold her in. Don't allow her to hesitate on point for a second, then rush in to flush the birds before you are ready. Talk to her, thus teaching her to focus on your voice and heed your instructions. When she holds a point and gives you time to reach her, pet her and praise her. Then move in to flush, shoot, and send her to fetch. If Jill points a robin or sparrow, that's okay; her scent discrimination will develop in time.

Many books have been written on this subject and this brief discussion is intended only to make you aware of some of the basic steps to be taken. If you hunt Jill regularly, you probably will want her professionally trained, or you will join a hunting club and take advantage of the instruction that is offered.

Field Trials

English bird-dog competition has been active since 1865, and field trials have been held in the United States since 1874. They are intended to prove the value of dogs in the performance of the duties for which they were bred. Dogs of similar heritage compete with one another under trial conditions. Field trial competition was very likely established to furnish bird-dog owners a means for comparing their dogs; the trials established bragging rights for the owner of "best dog."

Hunting-dog owners long ago recognized the importance of competition under a set of rules that was equal for all dogs and handlers. With standardized scoring, there is still some degree of interpretation that must be made by the judges, but by applying set rules to certain activities, the best dog usually will come out on top.

Early American field trials were open only to pointers and setters, and were a means of proving which bench show dogs of those breeds

A real life example of a Brittany successfully developing into a water retriever.

should be bred. A field trial was the only reliable way of separating the true bird dogs from the frill and fluff that were suspected to dominate bench shows. Field trial dogs came into their own in the 1940s, when the trials became more specialized, competition got stiffer, and professional handlers and trainers replaced owners and weekend shooters.

Brittanys were originally at a definite disadvantage, because trial judges were accustomed to judging dogs with long, feathered tails. Although Brittanys excelled as bird finders, they were routinely marked low in the "class" category.

In 1942 the American Brittany Club (ABC) formed and took charge of the all-Brittany field trials. In 1943, the AKC licensed its first Brittany field trial. The first AKC Field Champion and the first Dual Champion Brittany was Brit of Bellows Falls, who won those honors in 1946.

A Brittany holding his point for the hunter to ready for shooting.

ant, prairie chicken, chukar, and grouse-woodcock, and a Gun Dog Classic/Championship.

Field Trial Classes

Official AKC field trial classes are: Open Puppy, Open Derby, Gun Dog Stake, All-Age Stake, Limited Gun Dog Stake, and Limited All-Age Stake. They are separated by the dogs' ages and prior wins.

Amateur field trials attract many novices in the sport. If you wish more information about these trials, contact the Amateur Field Trial Clubs of America; you will find the address in the back of this book. For more information and Brittany field trial data, refer to Rheta Cartmell's *Book of the American Brittany*, published by the ABC and available from that organization. ABC and regional Brittany clubs will also furnish information regarding getting started in amateur field trial competition.

Hunting Tests

The AKC hunting test program for pointers was begun in 1985. This is a true testing program that complements formal field trials. The tests supply owners with another means to evaluate their bird dogs against official hunting standards without actual competition, as well as a rather informal and fun way to exhibit their dogs. Tests are judged by professionals and are intended to identify dogs that possess superior hunting abilities. Awards are made according to performance in the field under simulated, nearly natural hunting conditions.

Winners are awarded the AKC suffix titles of Junior Hunter (JH), Senior Hunter (SH), and

Field Champion

To be awarded a Field Champion title (FC), a dog must win ten points in judged trials. Points are awarded to the first-place winner in a regular stake competition. In the 1980s about 5,000 Brittanys competed in field trials. That competition produced about 700 Field Champions, and about one in five of those Field Champions possessed the coveted title of Dual Champion (DC). A Dual Champion is a dog that has been awarded the title of Champion of Record (Ch.) in AKC conformation shows, plus a Field Champion title in field trials. By December 2006, the recorded number of dual champion Brittanys was 508.

Brittany Nationals

The ABC holds National All Age Championships and National Gun Dog Championships annually, and a National Specialty Show, Summer Specialty Show, and three Futurities for both field and show. The ABC also sponsors a National Classic/Championship for quail, pheas-

Master Hunter (MH), which are added to the dogs' registered names.

Conformation Shows

Conformation competition (dog shows) often are called "beauty pageants" by those dog owners whose interests lie in other directions. However, that term isn't fair and doesn't quite cover the subject. Conformation shows are designed to promote registered purebred dogs and to identify breeding stock or potential breeding stock. To be eligible for showing, a dog must be intact, that is, not spayed or neutered. It must be free of hereditary diseases and deformities to the best of the judges' knowledge. In order to win in a show, the exhibited dog must be of the correct size, color, and markings. It must have the correct body type and amount of coat, and move with a sound and balanced gait.

The ideal Brittany is one that matches the breed standard written by the American Brittany Club and adopted by the AKC. Dog shows are designed to judge dogs of the same breed and sex against one another, and points are awarded for specific class wins, depending upon the number of competitors entered.

Titles

Having a dog that wins a prestigious title is a rewarding experience for the Brittany owner, but a feeling of accomplishment will come with every near miss as well. To own a dog that glides across the ring and receives the applause of the bystanders gives you a feeling of pride. To win is ecstasy!

The title Champion of Record (Ch.) is awarded to Jill when she earns 15 points, accumulated under at least three different judges in at least

A tired Brittany competitor returning from a grueling afternoon field trial.

three licensed shows. The number of points awarded with each win depends on the number of dogs against which she competed, cannot exceed five at any show, and must include two wins of no less than three points each (major wins). Only two dogs at each show earn points. To earn a Ch. is not as easy as it may sound!

Show Dogs

Any AKC-registered Brittany can be entered in a show provided that the dog has reached six months of age, is physically normal, and has been trained to behave in the ring. It must be manageable and trustworthy, since control is a vital part of participation in shows. The Brittany breed standard states that the dog should be happy and alert, neither mean nor shy.

A Brittany is not allowed in the conformation show ring if it has any disqualification that is listed in the standard. For the Brittany, that includes a size disqualification for a dog that is less than 17^1/$_2$ inches (44.5 cm) tall, or more than 20^1/$_2$ inches (52 cm) tall. A Brittany's nose pad (rubber) must be pigmented fawn, tan, brown, or pink. A black nose rubber is a disqualification. Another disqualification for Brittanys is any black color in its coat. A dog with one of those disqualifications is barred from future conformation shows.

If you are considering showing Jill, consult Brittany breeders in your local club. Have her *faulted*, or judged, by someone who has been in the ring. That person will point out any problems Jill may have, including immaturity, training, or conformation. If Jill appears to have winning qualities, enroll her in a conformation class. Enter

her in fun matches for experience (yours and hers). If all goes well in the classes and matches, you are ready for the big time. When you decide to enter her in a point show, you may exhibit her yourself or hire a professional handler.

A show dog and her handler must be trained. Jill must focus on her handler and obey directions given instantly. She can't be easily distracted, must stand very still when the judge runs his hands over her body, and she can't resent being gently lifted by the tail. The judge will open Jill's lips to expose her bite, and she must accept these invasions of privacy with good nature. A little tail wagging doesn't hurt her chances a bit.

Handlers

Specialty clubs and all-breed clubs usually hold handler classes at least annually. When the judge tells the handler "*Up and back,*" the reaction should be instantaneous. Sometimes judges call their top dogs out of competition very quietly, often with a hand gesture, and the handler must watch and listen carefully, because nothing is more embarrassing than having your dog chosen and not realizing it. No preference is given to child handlers, but a smiling, proud child handling a fine Brittany will quickly receive the judge's attention.

Breed Standard

Because of space limitations, the Official Standard for the Brittany is not presented here, but it can be obtained by writing to the American Brittany Club or the AKC, or it may be downloaded from the Internet.

A beautiful Brittany standing by for conformation judging in a dog show.

Brittanys all in a line for placement awarding in conformation competition.

Conformation Judging

AKC judges mentally compare each dog in the class with the *perfect* Brittany described in the standard. Allowances are made for age, maturity, and differences between the sexes. Brittanys are not judged on the basis of conformation alone. Judges must consider the individual dog's attitude, conditioning, training, and willingness. A dog that is happy and enjoying itself has a better chance at winning than one that is just going through the motions.

Types of Shows

There are two types of dog shows, specialty and all-breed events. Specialty shows are limited to dogs of a particular breed or group of similar breeds, and all-breed shows are unlimited, meaning that all registered dogs may be entered. Individual dog clubs manage the shows that are held under AKC rules with AKC judges.

Conformation Classes

There are five classes in which a dog may compete for points toward its championship. In all classes, males compete against other males, and bitches against other bitches.

- Puppy class, often divided into two groups: six to nine months and nine to 12 months
- Novice class
- Bred-by-Exhibitor class
- American-Bred class
- Open class

First the puppies are judged, then the Novice, Bred-by-Exhibitor, American-Bred, and Open. Classes are judged individually and the winning dogs from each class are brought back into the ring to compete again. That judging of first-place winners is called the Winners Class, and the winner of this class is called the Winners Dog. That dog receives championship points at the show.

The dog that placed second to the Winners Dog in its original male or female class is brought into the ring to compete with the other class winners for Reserve Winners Dog. If the Winners Dog is disqualified by the AKC for any reason, the Reserve Winners Dog receives the points.

The next class to be judged is made up of all entered Champions of Record (male and female), the Winners Dog, and the Winners Bitch. This is called the Best of Breed class, and

The hurdles are taken in stride by this Brittany at an agility trial.

A Brittany cautiously descending from the plank walk in an agility trial.

from it is selected the single animal that the judge considers the Best of Breed in the show. The judge next selects the Best of Winners from the Winners Dog and Winners Bitch. If one of those two dogs has already been selected as Best of Breed, that same dog is automatically named Best of Winners, and a Best of Opposite Sex is chosen from the class. Those awards end the judging in a specialty show.

In an all-breed show, the Best of Breed winner competes with other Best of Breed winners in its group. The seven Best of Group winners then compete against each other for the coveted Best in Show award.

Dogs that compete for field as well as conformation awards are considered "dual purpose"; the title of Dual Champion is awarded to dogs that have earned their Champion of Record title in conformation shows, in addition to a Field Champion title in field trials. That title designates a dog of superior conformation in which few faults were found. It is a talented hunter that has been judged against other field dogs and hasn't come away wanting. If your Brittany has earned other champion titles in other competitions, such as tracking, those titles are added to her name.

AKC titles are awarded to Jill only after many flawless performances in field trials, conformation shows, obedience, agility, or tracking—but you and I know that in her heart and in the hearts of her owners, every Brittany is a champion!

Obedience Trials

AKC Obedience Trials are formal competitions for all registered dogs regardless of breed or sex. An obedience trial is a competition that demonstrates the usefulness of the purebred

An energetic, well-trained Brittany taking the tunnel in an agility trial.

dog as a companion. All entries in each of the various obedience classes perform the same exercises in the same way and are scored by the judges. Each dog is awarded points according to its performance. The primary objective of an obedience trial is to prove the training and conditioning of a dog in every conceivable circumstance. Its purpose is to promote exemplary dog behavior in all situations, in public places and in the presence of other dogs and handlers.

This sport judges not only the training of the dog but its willingness to perform the work. In that regard, an obedience trial is very similar to a field trial. The dog must certainly be properly trained, but to do well, it must also show a certain "flair" or "class" when accomplishing the many tasks. A dog must be practiced and smooth, but the judges also look for a happy dog, not a robot.

Obedience Rules

There are many rules promulgated for the conduct and appearance of obedience dogs. Obedience trials are judged on performance and are not beauty contests. Spaying, castration, scars, or coat defects do not eliminate dogs from participation in obedience trials. However, lame or bandaged dogs cannot compete, and neither can dogs that have been dyed or artificially colored.

A handler can be excused from competition for many reasons, but handicapped handlers may compete in obedience trials. A judge will usually modify the rules to permit disabled handlers to participate, but their dogs must perform all the required exercises.

Obedience Classes and Awards

Obedience trials are divided into various classes, and each class has a different set of

This Brittany is descending from the elevated plank walk. He is focusing on the yellow-colored end that must be stepped upon.

from the AKC Web site. In essence, dogs are judged on their ability to follow a track that was plotted and laid out in the absence of all dogs and handlers.

Agility Trials

An agility trial is a true spectator sport, a fun event that boggles the minds of onlookers and brings excitement to all who attend. It demonstrates a dog's training, willingness, and energy as it works with its handler. Several levels of competition in agility trials are open to any AKC-registered dog. As in other AKC events (except conformation shows or field trials), no restrictions are placed on slight deviations from the breed standard or a neutered dog's participation. Various levels of competition are run, unique obstacles are mastered, points are awarded, and titles are earned at each level.

Good Citizen Certificate

Dog clubs throughout the United States administer Canine Good Citizen (CGC) tests. The AKC sponsors this very practical program, which is designed to promote good manners and exemplary behavior. A dog's evaluation is based on different activities that ensure that it is a good, trustworthy neighbor. No points are given and no title is earned, but a certificate is awarded for satisfactory performance. The scoring is a simple pass-fail evaluation for the entire set of tasks. However, a dog that fails the

competition rules. Certificates are awarded for winners of each class; the CD (Companion Dog) title is the coveted prize of every entry in the Novice class. Open class winners vie for the CDX (Companion Dog Excellent) title, and so forth. The ultimate accomplishment is a UDX (Utility Dog Excellent) title.

A Triple Champion is a dog that has earned a Field Champion title, a Champion of Record title, and an Obedience Trial Championship title.

Tracking Dog

Brittanys are also eligible to compete in AKC tracking tests. This is a sport in which Jill's excellent nose will prove quite valuable. Rules, levels, and awards for tracking are beyond the scope of this manual, but they can be obtained test may continue training and be tested again. The essential and easily taught tasks include allowing a stranger to approach, walking obediently on a loose leash, walking through a crowd, and sitting for examination by the judge. It considers the dog's reaction to a strange dog, to a distraction such as a door suddenly slamming, or a jogger running by.

AKC member clubs make CGC evaluations and information about them may be obtained by contacting the AKC or an all-breed club in your community. Having a Canine Good Citizen Certificate hanging on the wall is evidence that your Brittany has been trained. It also means that you love your dog enough to spend valuable time training it, and that Jill is a good neighbor.

A Brittany running through the agility trial hoops.

Therapy Dog

To discover another job for your Brittany, check out the Internet home pages of Therapy Dogs International or the Delta Society. Either of those two organizations will supply information relative to training and handling Jill in one of the most useful and gratifying endeavors you can imagine. A dog that qualifies and is certified is allowed entry into nursing homes, hospitals, and hospice homes to bring smiles and comfort to patients. If Jill is a typically outgoing, lovable, mature Brittany, she may bring a slice of happiness and peace to otherwise dull lives. Requirements are paraphrased below for Therapy Dogs International.

The dog must be in good health, tested and evaluated by a certified TDI evaluator, a minimum of one year of age, and have a sound, reliable temperament. It must possess an AKC Canine Good Citizen certificate and pass a tem- perament evaluation of suitability to become a therapy dog. That includes an evaluation of the dog's behavior around people who use some type of service equipment, like a wheelchair, walker, or crutches.

A Brittany taking the weave poles in stride.

HEALTH CARE

The most important factor in the life of your Brittany is not great beauty, super intelligence, or polished hunting abilities. Having a predictable attitude, an amiable disposition, and trainable character is getting closer. However, without good mental and physical health, he may be a disappointment. Health is the most valuable asset a house pet or competitor can possess.

Choosing a Good Veterinarian

Brittany ownership demands interaction with a wise animal-health professional, but how do you find one? Don't be afraid to shop around. Arrange an appointment with a local veterinarian before you buy your Brittany. A reliable, concerned professional will give you a few minutes of her or his time and will welcome your visit and inquiries. Ask about out-of-hours emergency needs, and if treatment for such situations is not offered in-house, discover who provides those services. Arrange for a tour of the animal hospital. Look at the facilities and equipment, noting its cleanliness and organization. Evaluate the dress and temperament of the veterinarian and staff. Are the personnel

This sound and beautiful Brittany is obviously in excellent health.

clean, friendly, caring, knowledgeable, and ready to share their knowledge with you?

Seek a veterinary clinician who has an open mind and is willing to listen to you, someone who will spend time explaining procedures and isn't too busy to tell you why a certain recommendation is made. Ask about the cost of spaying your female or castrating your male Brittany. Obtain a fee schedule or inquire about the charges for routine examinations, vaccinations, fecal exams, and worm treatment. Ask about heartworm, flea, and tick preventive plans and their cost.

If the veterinarian resists being interviewed, look for another. If she or he has no time for you as a prospective dog owner and client, how much more time will he or she have for your pet?

If possible, watch the veterinarian's tableside manner when handling an animal. Is the doctor in such a hurry that there is no time for small talk and a quick rub of a puppy's chin? Is he or

CHECKLIST

Home Evaluation of a Sick Brittany

✔ If you suspect that Chip isn't feeling well, take his rectal temperature. The normal range is from 101.5 to 102.5°F (38.5 to 39.5°C).

✔ Look at the color of his oral mucous membranes, which are normally bright pink. Dark or pale membranes may mean trouble.

✔ Check his breathing; it should be smooth and not labored.

✔ Take his pulse by pressing your finger against the inside of his thigh, about half way between his stifle and hip. A Brittany's normal heart rate is between 70 and 90 beats per minute.

✔ Look at his eyes; are the corneas bright, or dull? Are the whites red and inflamed? Is a discharge or pus evident?

✔ Has he been coughing or sneezing?

✔ When and what did he eat last?

✔ Have you seen his stool today, and if so, was it normal in color and consistency?

✔ Has he vomited in the recent past? If so, what did the vomitus look like? Was it bloody or mucoid? Did it contain foreign material?

✔ Is he lethargic or is he normally active? If he is lying around, does he respond to your voice and, if so, does he show any lameness?

Record your findings. If any were abnormal, call your veterinarian.

Caution: If you notice abnormal signs, don't wait a day or two to see if the dog gets better. Call your veterinarian!

she at ease in his/her role and comfortable with the pet?

The next step: Immediately after acquiring Chip, take him to your veterinarian for evaluation. Present the health documents that came with Chip and ask questions about future vaccination requirements. Obtain advice about parasite control and exotic diseases that may be endemic in your area. Discuss spaying or castration of your Brittany.

Immunization

The breeder usually begins immunizations soon after puppies are weaned. Vaccinations should be continued throughout Chip's life; however, a vaccination schedule should be specifically designed for him by his veterinarian after a thorough examination. It should consider his condition, age, and activities, as well as diseases prevalent in the region, and exposure potential.

Core vaccines: Core vaccines are advised by most authorities to be needed by most dogs in most regions of the United States. These vaccines are meant to prevent the following illnesses.

• Canine distemper (CD)
• Infectious canine hepatitis (CAV-2)
• Canine parvovirus (CPV)
• Rabies

Noncore vaccines: These may or may not be important to Chip's well-being but should be considered; the diseases they are meant to prevent are as follows.

• Canine parainfluenza virus (CPIV)
• Kennel cough (*Bordetella bronchiseptica*)
• Leptospirosis, or lepto (*Leptospira icterohemorrhagia*)
• Lyme disease (*Borrellia burgdorferi*)
• Giardia

• Canine coronavirus (vaccine available but not usually recommended)

Dog Diseases

Canine Distemper

This illness, also known as CD, dog plague, or hard pad, remains a significant threat to American canines. It kills many dogs, can't be cured, and is easily transmitted. It is caused by a virus that attacks the dog's respiratory tract, intestinal tract, and brain. The reservoir of infection for CD exists in stray-dog populations and wild carnivores such as coyotes, wolves, raccoons, and foxes.

Signs of CD may include fever, loss of appetite, lethargy, dehydration, diarrhea, and vomiting. A yellow or green ocular discharge and coughing are other signs of the disease. When young unvaccinated pups contract CD, they often die suddenly without displaying any symptoms. Permanent damage in those dogs that miraculously survive the disease includes hardened footpads, tooth enamel deficiencies, and neurological signs such as blindness or twitching of the extremities.

Infectious Canine Hepatitis

Known as ICH or CAV-2, this condition is caused by canine adenovirus-2, hence the abbreviation CAV-2. It is a systemic, usually lethal, liver infection that also destroys a puppy's resistance to other diseases. Signs of the disease are similar to those of CD, including the sudden death of unvaccinated puppies.

Leptospirosis

Also known as lepto, this devastating disease is carried by water rodents and is often spread by drinking contaminated river water. Its causative organisms are bacterialike microbes called spirochetes, which can destroy an affected dog's kidneys. Signs of lepto include lethargy, lack of appetite, thirst, rusty-colored urine, diarrhea, and vomiting, and affected dogs sometimes walk with a peculiar stilted, roach-backed gait.

Canine Parvovirus

Contagious and often fatal, this disease is easily spread via the feces of an affected dog. The virus is highly resistant to disinfectants and may survive for many months in dried dog feces. Signs are high fever, bloody diarrhea, vomiting, dehydration, and cardiac complications. Intensive therapy may be effective, but aftereffects may be significant.

Canine coronavirus is similar to parvo in that both can cause bloody diarrhea and vomiting, general malaise, and death in many affected puppies or adults.

Rabies

Rabies is a fatal systemic neurological disease that can affect all warm-blooded animals, including humans. The virus invades the salivary glands of an infected animal and paralyzes the throat. It is transmitted from one animal to another through infected saliva and frequently follows a bite wound. Reservoirs of the rabies virus are found in wild animals such as coyotes, skunks, raccoons, bats, rats, ferrets, and mink. The virus also occurs in domestic animals such as cattle, dogs, and cats. If a human is bitten by a rabid animal, immediate medical treatment is necessary to stop the infection.

Lyme Disease

This disease is spread by blood-sucking parasites, typically deer ticks, that are the vectors,

honking cough that may continue for many weeks. No specific therapy will cure kennel cough, but ignoring it may lead to pneumonia.

Valley Fever

Caused by the fungus *Coccidioides immitus,* valley fever can be fatal. The disease is usually diagnosed in desert regions of the southwestern United States. Windborne, microscopic fungal spores are nearly indestructible and remain dormant in the soil for eons but become a problem when they are ingested or inhaled by a receptive host. Upon invasion, the organism springs to life, rapidly reproduces, and may cause lethargy, joint pain, tenderness, lameness, lung involvement that results in respiratory distress, and a plethora of other signs. The disease is sometimes difficult to diagnose, very difficult to treat, and often requires many months of therapy.

Canine Influenza

Canine influenza is reported to be a new disease of dogs. It was studied in Florida early in 2004 in racing Greyhounds and has apparently spread to other states. It is somewhat like kennel cough and may be fatal if not treated appropriately. In its usual and milder form, respiratory signs may be seen for about three weeks before recovery. Its spread is rapid by aerosol from sneezing and coughing, thus flu often is seen where dogs are concentrated, such as Greyhounds or other closely kenneled dogs. No vaccine is available at this time and no spread to humans has been documented. Your veterinarian can send blood samples from suspected dogs to a laboratory for positive identification.

or carriers, for *Borrellia* bacteria. The infection causes nonspecific, generalized pain, fever, joint pain and swelling, lymph node swelling, and vague generalized illness. Lyme disease may affect humans.

Ehrlichiosis is another serious tick-borne disease, transmitted by the brown dog tick. It is manifested by nosebleeds, swelling of the limbs, anemia, and a multitude of other signs. It can be fatal if not treated early and adequately.

Kennel Cough

In its simplest form kennel cough is not fatal. It is spread by airborne particles, often from the sneezes and coughing of an infected dog. It frequently is caused by a combination of bacterial and viral pathogens such as *Bordetella* bacteria and parainfluenza virus. It causes a chronic,

Gastric Dilatation and Volvulus (GDV)

This condition primarily affects giant breeds but is occasionally seen in smaller dogs. It can be fatal if not recognized promptly and treated aggressively. GDV may be associated with several factors.

- Dogs with big appetites that consume their food voraciously.
- Feeding a single, large meal each day.
- Feeding dry, unmoistened kibble.
- Allowing free access to water immediately following meals.
- Exercising within an hour of a big meal.

Note: Interestingly, a Purdue University study suggests that dogs with happy, well-adjusted temperaments are less apt to develop GDV than those that are nervous and stressed.

GDV is always a dire, potentially fatal emergency and immediate veterinary intervention is critical. It usually begins two to six hours after eating a large meal. Its signs include:

- Frequent, unproductive retching.
- Bloating, especially on the left side behind the rib cage.
- Dyspnea (difficult breathing) and stringy saliva drooling from the mouth.
- Dark mucous membrane color.
- Staggering, loss of balance, coughing attempts.

Caution: Death may follow within an hour of onset of the symptoms. If GDV is suspected, contact an emergency veterinary clinic immediately!

Grass Awns

The bearded seed pods that catch in your socks when you walk though the grass may be much more significant when encountered by your Brittany. The tiny bearded awns can penetrate the webs between Chip's toes and migrate deeply into his feet, or they may make their

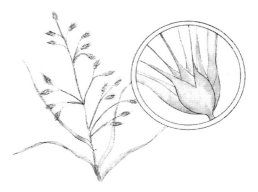

A sharp little awn can cause trouble if it works down into the ear canals or sticks between the dog's toes.

way into Chip's ear canals, causing great discomfort, infection, and necessitating a trip to your veterinarian for removal.

Parasites

Parasite control is becoming more complex each year. A veterinarian who practices in your area knows which parasites are present and what products you can use for safe, effective, and commonsense control. Several products are available that control different parasites in a single medication. Some are oral preparations and others are applied to Chip's skin. But many hoaxes and antiquated methods of parasite control also exist. Don't attempt to diagnose, treat, or prevent parasites without expert advice. No worm medication exists that is universally effective, and an especially perilous procedure is to "worm" all puppies, whether or not a parasite infestation has been diagnosed.

Tip: There is no excuse for doing something well that shouldn't be done at all.

This Brittany in the field is demonstrating its skill as a retriever.

Endoparasites (Internal Parasites)

These can live within Chip's body at his expense.

Roundworm larvae can infest unborn puppies from their dam. After whelping, the larvae migrate through the puppies' tissues, reach the lungs, are coughed up, swallowed, and the adult roundworms start their life cycle all over again. Roundworm eggs pass out in the pup's feces and spread to other dogs.

Hookworm is a microscopic blood-sucking intestinal parasite that can cause anemia and pain to its hosts. Hookworm eggs pass out of the gut and hatch into larvae, which penetrate the skin of hosts, migrate through the host's body, reach the intestine, and finish their life cycle.

Tapeworm is a two-host parasite. An adult tapeworm attaches its head (scolex) to the lining of the dog's gut and its segmented body grows to great lengths. Segments break off, pass from the gut, and are consumed by secondary hosts such as fleas or larger animals, like deer. A dog consumes the tissues of the secondary host, which contains a tapeworm cyst. The cyst wall digests and hundreds of scoleces emerge.

Heartworm is a threat to all American dogs. An adult heartworm grows to many inches in length, lives within the heart's chambers or large blood vessels, and produces living larvae. The presence of heavy heartworm infestation can seriously compromise the host's heart. When a mosquito sucks blood from an infested dog, the larvae of the heartworm, *Dirofilaria immitus,* are picked up by the insect and are injected into new hosts.

This picture-perfect Brittany is standing on point.

Ectoparasites (External Parasites)

These live on a Brittany's skin. They are usually diagnosed by skin scraping or culture and are treated with topical or systemic medication.

Mites are microscopic, eight-legged parasites that burrow beneath and within the skin. They cause hair loss, inflammation, itching, and serum oozing. There are several genera of mites, each of which prefers a different region of a host's body. *Cheyletiella, Demodex, Psoroptes*, and *Sarcoptes* are diagnosed by viewing a skin scraping under a microscope. Ear mites (*Otodectes*) may parasitize Chip's ear canals and are diagnosed by examining his ear wax.

Fungus (*Microsporum canis*) infestations are found on Chip's belly skin and appear as circular, raised red lesions, hence the common name, ringworm.

Fleas are extremely common and their control must receive your undivided attention. A flea is a tiny white insect that lives part-time both on a host's body and in the host's environment. Flea infestations are prevalent in warm, high-humidity regions of southeastern America but may be a problem anywhere except, perhaps, in mountainous and cool climates. A flea bites its host and laps the oozing serum, its saliva often causing allergic inflammation and itching. Adult fleas are often found on your Brittany's back, where you might see dozens of them hopping about on his fur. Adult fleas mate and lay eggs, which drop and molt on the ground or floor. The flea larvae eat organic material, including tapeworm segments. After several molts, the adult flea emerges and seeks a viable host, and the whole cycle begins

A Brittany holding a point in a cornfield.

again. Caution: A dog flea can use a human for its host!

Biological control programs have been devised that involve an application to your yard, using tiny nematodes (worms) that consume flea eggs but are harmless to humans and pets. Other controls involve the use of insect growth regulator hormones that interfere with the flea's life cycle. Do not use oral medication, dips, sprays, powders, medicated collars, or other drugs that are not labeled for the specific age and weight of your Brittany.

Lice dwell permanently on the skin and feed on the blood of their hosts, but they are readily controlled. A louse lays its white eggs, called

TIP

Removing a Tick

To remove a tick, put on a pair of latex or nitrile gloves. Dampen Chip's hair with alcohol, and grasp the tick as close as possible to its skin attachment with a pair of blunt tweezers or hemostat forceps. Slowly pull the tick out, using gentle but firm pressure. Drop the tick into a vial of alcohol but don't handle it with bare fingers, don't crush it, don't toss it on the ground or into a wastebasket, and don't burn it

nits, sticking them on the dog's hair, where they can be found with the aid of a magnifying glass.

Ticks can be seen with your naked eye. The female tick buries her head in the host's skin and sucks blood, which causes her body to swell to the size of a grape. Male ticks are tiny and may be found attached to the host's skin alongside the female. The engorged female drops to the ground or floor and lays thousands of eggs, which hatch and molt twice to become adults. Each of the three life stages of the tick must suck blood from a host in order to progress to the next stage. Most ticks require multiple hosts, usually of different species—one for the adult, one for the larva, and one for the nymph. The hardest tick to control is *Rhipcephalus sanguineus,* or brown dog tick. All forms of that parasite feed on canine blood. Ticks act as vectors for various diseases such as Lyme disease. After the tick is removed, clean the skin lesion that remains with alcohol twice daily for a few days to prevent infection.

This old Brittany will benefit from some tender geriatric care.

Old Brittanys

Old friends need special health accommodations and medical plans, which should include:
• Two professional physical exams a year, possibly accompanied by laboratory screens.
• Several pads around the house to lie on.
• A ramp up the back-porch stairs.
• Anti-inflammatory arthritis drugs for joint pain.
• Special vision health considerations when cataracts form.
• Help when getting up.
• Fresh drinking water supplied in various places throughout the house.
• Regular, slower, shorter walks.
• More frequent, smaller meals.

Euthanasia

When all medication and special considerations have failed and Chip's future holds nothing but pain and confusion, allow your old buddy an easy end to life. That final act of kindness will be appreciated! Ask your veterinarian to visit you at home or to allow you to bring Chip to the clinic before opening or after closing. Euthanasia is accomplished by an intravenous injection that ends his life painlessly, quickly, and easily. Stay with him, reassure and comfort him, and trust the competence of your veterinarian. Join a group of people who have had similar experiences. Plant a tree to commemorate Chip's life, and face your sorrow as he would have wanted you to.

WHY NOT TO BREED YOUR BRITTANY

If you are seriously considering breeding your Brittany, be aware that purebred dog breeding is not a lucrative business. It is fraught with pitfalls that usually discourage and disappoint those who try it. Only Brittanys that have proven to be flawless in competition, in virtually every capacity, should be bred.

The Best of the Best?

Jill is a winner! She is a wonderful family pet, companion, and hunting dog, but those features were why you bought a Brittany. Examine your motives for breeding. Are you really dedicated to breed Jill because her litter would improve the breed? Is she the best by test?

Brittany breeding involves competition against the finest of the fine, and that means having a nearly perfect Brittany in every feature. It also means that you must spend countless hours of your time and loads of money on classes, training, and competing against the very best Brittanys in dog shows and other events.

Spayed Brittanys are usually healthy and easy to care for.

Important Considerations

Two things you definitely need to undertake breeding your dog are a big bankroll and loads of dedication! Consider the following:

• A breeding Brittany must be proven clear of congenital diseases such hip dysplasia and progressive retinal atrophy.

• More costs are incurred proving her conformation, including entry fees, training, handler's fees, and travel.

• Costs are significant for providing health and dietary care for a brood bitch and her litter. Check the cost of her prenatal exam, post-whelping exam, possible X-ray and ultrasound imaging, as well as the expense of a potential caesarean section.

• Think about a whelping box, puppy food, and vaccinations.

A neutered Brittany doesn't lose interest in field work.

• Consider the time you will have to spend cleaning up after a litter for several weeks as well as seeking good homes for the puppies.
• Pyometra and mammary cancer are very prevalent, possibly fatal, diseases common to unspayed bitches.

Responsible Ownership

After seeing and admiring a well-trained Brittany and duly noting its beautiful personality and superb intelligence, a naïve person might assume that all Brittanys somehow automatically grow up with those features. Expanding on that artless assumption, such a person purchases a Brittany puppy without investigating the patience, time, and work required to train it. A year later the dog has become a nuisance, a liability that results from no fault of its own.

Lack of planning has led to the destruction of millions of wonderful canine pets that were obtained without thought by well-meaning families. Unfortunately, every breed is occasionally caught up in this scenario and winds up in the dog warden's truck or in a rescue organization. Rejected, unwanted pets now number in the hundreds of thousands in the United States. They occupy dog pounds, breed rescue services, and animal shelters across the country. When those facilities can no longer house them, they are euthanized ("put to sleep") in enormous numbers.

Controlling Overpopulation

Only responsible dog owners and breeders can control canine overpopulation. That includes all of us who obtain dogs and don't have them sexually neutered before they reach reproductive age. Nearly as irresponsible are those of us who adopt a dog and fail to train it, teach it manners, and keep it occupied. We must accept the role of steward when we acquire a dog. That is critically important, whether shopping for a purebred, trainable Brittany, a mixed-breed pup, or a shelter rescue.

Dog breeders should employ a neutering policy for all pets sold; written contracts can be used to ensure that the policy is followed. All prospective dog breeders should be aware that only the best examples of their chosen breed should be used in a breeding program. Irresponsible owners who assume that all registered dogs are of breeding quality exacerbate the dog overpopulation problem.

If you find yourself with a Brittany that you can't keep, contact the Brittany club in your area or the American Brittany Club. There is also a Brittany rescue association that will help you deal with your problem. E-mail addresses are provided at the back of this book.

Spaying and Neutering

Spaying

Spaying is a surgical ovariohysterectomy, or removal of the uterus and ovaries. Please note: This procedure does *not* affect the bitch's hunting ability, temperament, personality, or trainability. Some good reasons to spay a female before her first heat are that it:
• prevents three-week estrous (heat) cycles twice a year;
• prevents the possibility of accidental breeding;
• solves several nuisance problems (a bitch in heat attracts male dogs of the neighborhood to your door, for example);

TIP

Obesity and Spaying or Neutering

Spaying a female or neutering a male doesn't cause obesity. Brittanys get fat for the same reasons people do: They consume more calories than their bodies burn. Most obesity problems result from overfeeding, but medical reasons also exist that cause dogs to store their calories. If Jill becomes overweight, take her to your veterinarian for diagnosis. If she's just normal but fat, begin a logical course of nutritional management.

• eliminates the bloody discharge Jill would have while in season (which could spoil carpets, for example);
• may calm a nervous bitch.

Neutering (Castration)

Neutering (castrating) a male dog means surgical removal of both testicles. Please note: Neutering a male at any age does not reduce his hunting ability or cause adverse changes in temperament, personality, or trainability. Reasons for castrating a young male are nearly as important as the reasons for spaying a female; see the following list.
• A castrated male is often less aggressive and quieter.
• Prostate cancer and testicular tumors do not occur in a castrated male.
• A castrated male is happy and content to stay at home and won't jump the fence to find a female in heat.

Books

Alderton, David. *Dogs*. New York: DK Publishing, Inc., 1993.

American Kennel Club. *The Complete Dog Book*. 20th ed. New York: Ballantine Books, 2006.

Beaver, Bonnie V. *Canine Behavior*. Philadelphia: W. B. Saunders Company, 1999.

Cartmell, Rheta. *The Book of the American Brittany*. Aledo, TX: American Brittany Club, Inc., 1980.

Clark, Ross, and Joan Stainer. *Medical & Genetic Aspects of Purebred Dogs*. Fairway, KS: Forum Publications, Inc., 1994.

Coile, D. Caroline. *Encyclopedia of Dog Breeds*. 2nd ed. Hauppauge, NY: Barron's Educational Series, Inc., 2005.

Davis, Henry. *The Modern Dog Encyclopedia*. Harrisburg, PA: Stackpole Company, 1958.

Dee, Larry, et. al. *Encyclopedia of Dog Health and Care*. New York: Philip Lief Group, Inc., 1994.

Fields-Babineau, Miriam. *Dog Training with a Head Halter*. Hauppauge, NY: Barron's Educational Series, Inc., 2000.

Lorenz, Michael, and Larry Cornelius. *Small Animal Medical Diagnosis*. 2nd ed. Philadelphia: J. B. Lippincott, 1993.

Riddle, Maxwell. *The New Complete Brittany*. New York: Howell Book House, 1987.

Verhoef-Verhallen, Esther J. J. *Encyclopaedia of Dogs*. Lisse, The Netherlands: Rebo Productions, 1996.

Von der Leyen, Katharina. *140 Dog Breeds*. Hauppauge, NY: Barron's Educational Series, Inc., 2000.

Yamazaki, Tetsu, and Toyoharu Kojima. *Legacy of the Dog*. San Francisco: Chronicle Books, 1995.

Web Sites

Amateur Field Trial Clubs of America
www.aftca.org

American Brittany Club
clubs.akc.org/brit/
(Click on *Inside ABC* for breed standard, lists of officers, regional clubs, and ABC and AKC forms.)

American Brittany Rescue
www.americanbrittanyrescue.org

American Kennel Club
www.akc.org

Orthopedic Foundations for Animals
offa.org/hipinfo.html

Canine Eye Registration Foundation
vmdb.org/cerf.html

This Brittany is focusing on an unseen bird in the cover.

A Brittany on point and concentrating on business.

INDEX

About the Author

During his years of veterinary practice, Dr. Rice gained a unique understanding of the relationship between hunting dogs and their owners and the special needs of both. Brittanys were favorites of his on the exam table and in the field. Writing was a hobby during his professional life, and after retiring he embarked on a serious writing career. By reading and researching purebred dog breeds, he maintains his knowledge of the dog fancy. In addition to this second edition of his book on Brittanys, his writing efforts for Barron's include these titles. *Bullmastiffs*; *Bengal Cats* (1st and 2nd eds.); *Akitas* (1st and 2nd eds.); *Spaniels* (2nd ed.); *Small Dog Breeds*; *West Highland White Terriers*; *Big Dog Breeds*; *The Beagle Handbook*; *The Dog Handbook*; *Chesapeake Bay Retrievers*; *The Well-Mannered Cat*; *Dogs from A to Z*; *Training Your German Shepherd Dog*; *Complete Book of Cat Breeding*; and *Complete Book of Dog Breeding*.

Acknowledgments

My sincere gratitude goes out to the management and editorial staff at Barron's Educational Series for giving me the opportunity to bring *Brittanys* up to date. I especially thank my editor, Anne McNamara, for guiding me through this second edition in its new format. And as always, I'm greatly indebted to my wife, Marilyn, for her expert proofreading and patience while I've been glued to this infernal machine for months at a time (I love it!).

Important Note

This pet owner's manual tells the reader how to buy or adopt, and care for a Brittany. The author and publisher consider it important to point out that the advice given in the book is meant primarily for normally developed dogs of excellent physical health and sound temperament.

Anyone who acquires a fully-grown dog should be aware that the animal has already formed its basic impressions of human beings. The new owner should observe the animal carefully, including its behavior toward humans, and, whenever possible, should meet the previous owner.

Caution is further advised in the association of children with dogs, in meeting with other dogs, and in exercising the dog without a leash.

Even well-behaved and carefully supervised dogs can sometimes damage property or cause accidents. It is therefore in the owner's interest to be adequately insured against such eventualities, and we strongly urge all dog owners to purchase a liability policy that also covers their dog.

Photo Credits

Kent Akselsen: 76, 77 (bottom), 92, and 93; Norvia Behling: 21 and 60; Kent Dannen: 34; Tara Darling: 6, 12 (top and bottom), 16, 18, 36 (top), 42, 74 (bottom), 78, and 90; Cheryl Ertelt: 36 (bottom), 64, 73, 77 (top), 79, and 88; Jean M. Fogle: 7, 11, 23, 24, 30, 31, 37, 39, 43, 46, 53, 54, 57 (top left), 58, 63, 68, 70, 71, 74 (top), 75, 85, 86, and 89; Isabelle Francais: 4, 9, 10, 13, 15, 17, 22, 35, 38, 40, 41, 44, 45, 56, 59, 61 (top and bottom), 62 (top and bottom), and 87; Pets by Paulette: 72; Judith E. Strom: 2–3, 5, 8, 20, 28, 29, 47, 50, 51, 57 (top right), 65, 66, 67, 69, 82, and 84.

Cover Photos

All photos by Kent Akselsen.

© Copyright 2008, 1998 by Barron's Educational Series, Inc.

All inquiries should be addressed to:
Barron's Educational Series, Inc.
250 Wireless Boulevard
Hauppauge, NY 11788
www.barronseduc.com

ISBN-13: 978-0-7641-3772-3
ISBN-10: 0-7641-3772-7

Library of Congress Catalog Card No. 2007005006

Library of Congress Cataloging-in-Publication Data
Rice, Dan, 1933-
    Brittanys : everything about history, purchase, care, nutrition, training, and behavior / Dan Rice ; filled with full-color photographs, illustrations by Michele Earle-Bridges.
        p. cm.
    Includes bibliographical references and index.
    ISBN-13: 978-0-7641-3772-3
    ISBN-10: 0-7641-3772-7
    1. Brittany spaniel. I. Title.

SF429.B78R5   2008
636.752—dc22   2007005006

Printed in China
9 8 7 6 5 4 3 2 1